10687927

THE MYSTICS

The Dial Press

New York   1974

Aubrey Menen

THE MYSTICS

Photographs by Graham Hall

Contents

The purpose of the book

I have written this book for those who have wished to know something of Hindu mysticism but who have been repelled by the fudge which surrounds it.

The fudge is a pity, but it probably cannot be helped. The honest sort of Indian mystic has something very simple to say. He knows a way of putting our minds to rest without resorting to drink, or drugs, or a crack over the head with a hammer. It is a way of stopping you thinking. It has no appeal to people whose worry is that they never seem to have started: but more intelligent people do often feel that they need a holiday from their own minds, while leaving them intact to come home to when the holiday is over.

That is all Indian mysticism is about, but, as I shall show in this book, it is quite enough. In fact, it is one of the most revolutionary ideas in the history of civilization.

And that is the trouble. One of its most trustworthy exponents, J. Krishnamurti, has put the thing very neatly. 'Most of us', he says, 'want to be terribly respectable.' Indian mysticism is founded on the Upanishads. These are essays on what we would nowadays call psychology which were inserted into the ancient sacred texts of the Hindus. They are sometimes very beautiful to read, but they are not respectable at all. The sages who gave rise to them were aware of this, and said, in a half-hearted way, that perhaps their doctrine discovery should not be spread too much: certainly not to fools.

Now India has always had its fair measure of fools, but as to respectability, the measure is pressed down and flowing over. For about two millennia, the Upanishadic teaching has been a source of embarrassment to the respectable: hence the fudge, or rather I should say, the gigantic intellectual fig-leaf which has been spread over it.

A rational man, investigating the teaching, comes almost immediately upon daunting contradictions. I shall give many of them in what follows, but I shall start off with one.

The sages of the Upanishads were quite clear. When the mind is shut off, it has no thoughts and no emotions, not even the shadowy and fleeting emotions one has in a dream. It is therefore disconcerting to find saffron-robed swamis and gurus* describing this as a state of *bliss*.

'Bliss' is a vague word in English or in any other language, including Sanskrit. But one thing is sure about it: it describes an emotion. Then how can it be used to describe a state in which you feel no emotion? It cannot. But it *is* used, and it puts many an enquirer off further research. There are a lot of people who would look with suspicion on being made, willy-nilly, blissful, especially in the West. It reminds them too much of a nun in rapt communion with God. Unfortunately the sages of the Upanishads were open atheists and (sometimes quite coarsely) against organized religion.

In explaining all this, I promise the reader that I shall not urge him to tie his semi-nude body into knots. This will not help to put the mind to rest at all, although it may put the body to rest for a week with a severe backache. I shall not insist, like so many Indian gurus, that the reader can attain enlightenment only by becoming a vegetarian, for the true basis of this teaching is that Hindus are finicky about their food, and gurus, like the rest of us, feel a nostalgia for mother's cooking. I shall describe these vagaries, for they are sometimes diverting, but by and large I shall stick to the original teaching, as, indeed, do the new breed of gurus who have arisen in recent years.

First, I shall go deep into history: without a knowledge of that, nothing Indian can be understood. Next, I shall portray the great forerunners – Sankara, Ramakrishna, Vivekananda, the men who gave shape to the modern mystics. Lastly, I shall come down to our own times. I aim to provide the Western enquirer, sceptic or not, with the means to distinguish the charlatan, whose aim is to deceive him, from the honest teacher, whose only object is to help.

*A swami is one versed in the ancient texts: a guru is a personal teacher.

Ganesh, one of the most popular gods of orthodox Hinduism. The son of Shiva and Parvati, he was born after they had seen elephants copulating. He brings good luck and removes obstacles. >

(Overleaf) Statues of Ganesh are kept in the home. During his ten-day festival, he is taken to the sea and immersed in the water. Then a new statue is bought.

The organized Hindu

About two thousand years before the birth of Christ a tribe living near the Aral Sea in Russia emigrated southwards. At one point the tribe broke up into two parts. One turned West and may have been the ancestors of all the Greeks: another turned East to India, and are certainly *not* the ancestors of all the Indians. There were Indians already there, and their descendants are in India today.

The invaders called themselves 'Aryans', which means 'noble': the original inhabitants called themselves a wide variety of names, which we nowadays lump together for convenience under the name 'Dravidians'. The Aryans had a fair skin, fair hair and blue eyes. The Dravidians had black hair, a deep brown complexion and dark eyes.

The complexion of the Aryans was the colour of oatmeal. It was quite obvious to them that it was better to have an oatmeal face than a brown one. An oatmeal face, they further argued, was a sign that they were racially superior to the Dravidians, whom, to drive the point home, they called 'black'.

Unfortunately for this view, the Aryans were not superior to the blacks. They were way behind them. The blacks had towns; the Aryans were so far from having them they did not even have a word to describe them, so they borrowed one from the blacks. The blacks could build with bricks, which the Aryans could not. They had fortresses which gave the superior invaders a good deal of trouble: they knew a great deal about agriculture, which the Aryans, who were a pastoral people, had to learn.

It was thus clear to the Aryans that the blacks should be kept in their place and that place, preferably, should be as low in the social scale as possible. It should not be forgotten that it was this racial prejudice which gave rise, by devious paths, to the Upanishads. I do not mean that the Upanishadic sages liked the colour of oatmeal, or that they thought that black was beautiful. On the contrary, they taught that the whole thing was nonsense.

< *In Vedic times, the Aryans worshipped nature gods. The principal one was Indra, god of the weather, of lightning and thunder, and of rain. This photograph shows the onset of the monsoon of 1972. After a good start, it failed, bringing starvation and destitution to millions, underlining the vital importance of the weather to both Aryans and modern Indians.*

The Aryans conquered a good deal of north India, while the Dravidians held the south. Each of the two had its own religion. The Aryans worshipped a nature god called Indra, who could control thunderstorms and, most importantly, the rainfall. A lesser God, Varuna, was more concerned with morals and good behaviour. The Aryans worshipped their gods by praying to them, singing hymns to them (some very beautiful to read even today) and by getting drunk. Their intoxicant was something called Soma, and although there is a general idea among young people today that this was a drug, the truth is that we have not the faintest idea of what it really was.

The Dravidians had their own gods, but we are very vague as to who they were. We only know that the Aryans thought their religious practices were disgusting. Curiously, one of these practices was Yoga.

In the early days of the Aryan conquest, they were their own priests. The male head of each house conducted the daily worship in his own courtyard, the family attending. Along with the hymns and the prayers, he recited a series of spells which were thought to have the effect of binding the god to do the worshippers' will. These were called *mantras*. It is interesting to reflect that these spells are still recited in gatherings of Indian mystics from California to New Delhi. Hymns, prayers and mantras were gathered together, long afterwards, in a book called the Rig-Veda.

Hindus today regard the Rig-Veda with great reverence, although the religion which it served has quite disappeared, along with Indra and Varuna. Hinduism is largely the product of the despised blacks, one of whose gods was an early form of Krishna, of whom we shall have much to say in what follows.

Now the blacks were handsome. Indians still are; if you tell them so, they take it as a matter of course. Inevitably some of the oatmeals had sex with them, and soon the master-race found it had a number of members who were the un-orthodox colour of milk chocolate.

This made the Aryans feel insecure. We can well understand it. The Nazis, who also called themselves Aryans, felt so uncertain of themselves that they killed off some six million Jews. That is one of the most extraordinary facts of history. I now have to tell of another which, while not as drastic, is equally strange.

We have seen that at first the householders were their own priests and them-selves said the magic incantations that forced the gods to keep things bowling along in the right direction. But as the Aryans moved from a pastoral way of life to that of settled tillers of the soil, the spells grew more numerous. Besides, as every child knows, spells do not work unless you get the words exactly right

One of Shiva's guardians (from Elephanta); all orthodox Hindu belief is populated by thousands of semi-divine figures. >

Brahmins at left and right can be identified by the sacred threads around their shoulders.

and say them in the right tone of voice. Only witches can do that, and it is this skill which makes them so powerful.

The Aryans developed a whole tribe of witches, or rather wizards, for they were all male. These male witches were the Brahmins. They were known as 'the twice-born'. Their first birth was when they left the womb: their second was when, in boyhood, they were invested with a three-fold thread which hung from one shoulder across the body to the waist. Hindu priests wear it to this day.

The Aryans believed that only those thread-wearers could say the spells in the right way. They were a trade-union of wizards, and the union was a firmly closed shop. No one could join it who had not been fathered by a Brahmin.

They slowly grew into a powerful aristocracy, even more powerful than the kings themselves. A king ruled with the permission of the gods; but the gods were permissive only at the request of the Brahmins, so the Brahmins became king-makers and, should occasion arise, king-disposers.

To preserve their immense power, the Brahmins set up a social system which is unique in history. They divided all their subjects into four categories, with a

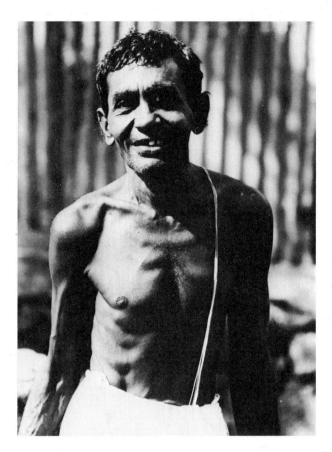 

rag-bag to hold those who could not be fitted in. At the top was themselves. They did no work, except to say the spells and prayers and make the daily sacrifices. They laid down that they should be revered, fed, clothed and handsomely re-warded by the rest of the community. Next came the kings, and the warriors who defended the land – the dukes, marquesses, and knights of the Western feudal system. After them, and always downwards in importance, were the farmers, merchants and such – the people who did the better class of work. Below them, last and, emphatically, least, were the common labourers. These, significantly, were called 'black', from which it may be deduced that they included a large number of the original inhabitants of the land, who were thus, at last, put in their place. Beyond these four divisions was a group which was put completely outside the pale of society. Slaves, scavengers, workers in unclean professions, and the more primitive of the Dravidians made up this unhappy band.

These five groups were dragooned by the Brahmins in a manner which no totalitarian dictator has dared to copy. Nobody could change his group. He could not move upwards. But he could tumble downwards: if he disobeyed the rules

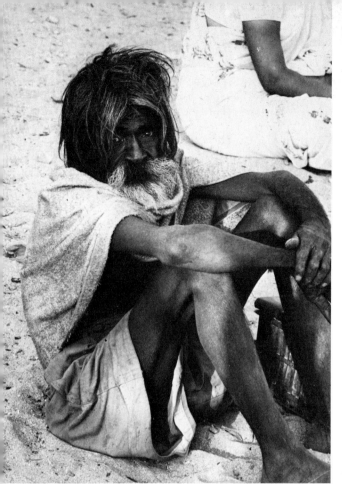

Untouchables or Harijans (Mahatma Gandhi renamed them 'The People of God').
Though the new Indian constitution grants them equal rights, they remain poor and
oppressed by the higher castes.

which the Brahmin promulgated, he could be thrown out of his group, to join
the rabble at, or beneath, the bottom. He was forbidden to marry outside his
class, and he was even forbidden to eat with anyone who was not in his group.
As for the ones who were pushed outside the system, their very presence was held
to be defiling, much less their touch. They had to keep a fixed number of yards
away from any of the four groups: where there was a walled town, they were
kept outside.

Nothing like this social organization has been known outside India. There are
some resemblances to it in Plato's monstrous Republic but that, fortunately, has
remained imaginary. I have been describing, of course, the caste system. The
five divisions were named the Brahmins, the Kshatriyas, the Vaisyas, the Sudras,
and the Untouchables. The sages of the Upanishads, I am happy to say, came from
all the classes, as their followers do today.

ORTHODOX HINDUISM
*The Shri Vyangtesh Balagi temple in Bombay. (The Hindi inscription
above the door is its name.)*

Part of the pagoda of Mahalaxmi temple in Bombay.

Having imposed this sentence of universal imprisonment on the people, the Brahmins took the bit between their teeth. They drew up regulations which controlled in the minutest detail the life of a man, woman and child. Apart from decreeing the innumerable religious acts which the citizen was required to pay the Brahmin to perform, rules were laid down as to when and how he should go to bed with his wife, what he should eat, how he should pass water and defecate, how he should run his house and his business, and how he should bring up his children to live their lives out in the same way.

This mass of regulations was gathered together sometime between 600 BC and AD 300 into a code of twelve books and 100,000 verses by a law-giver called Manu. He may have been a mythical character, but his code is very real. It controlled Hindu life for a longer period than any other body of laws in the history of mankind. It lasted down to modern times, and some of its injunctions still weigh with the orthodox.

To the orthodox Hindu, the cow is sacred and may not be killed. The origin of the belief is obscure but it may have come from Egypt, where the cow represented heaven.

Above. The stories of the gods are often performed by travelling troupes of actors, sometimes children.

Below. The Hindu gods may be worshipped anywhere. Wayside shrines, like the one below, are to be found throughout the country; devotion consists of saying a prayer and throwing down some money.

So far I have given the classical view of the Brahminical organization of society: that is, that they created four divisions of the people, with a fifth outside the system. But from our perspective, at the closing decades of the twentieth century, we can see that they set up a sixth caste – that of women.

It would seem from the Rig-Veda that before the Brahmin ascendancy women held an honourable position in society. They could perform certain prescribed rites of worship – something they still cannot do among large sections of Christian believers. Some sacrifices, such as that ensuring a good harvest, or finding a good husband for the daughters, were their exclusive province. They even composed some of the hymns.

The Brahmins destroyed all this with a ferocity which sometimes slides into the pathological. The Laws of Manu point to women as the root of all evil. That is something, it is true, which has been said before and since, in other climes. But here the abuse of women is unparalleled. She is considered to be of the lowest of the four castes, whatever the status of her husband. He may not eat with her, though she is given gracious permission to eat his leavings. Killing a low-caste person is considered a light crime: killing a woman is not a whit more serious:

Orthodox Hinduism includes private family rites. In these three pictures a mother is offering food to the gods; her white sari indicates that she is a widow.

25

Hindu worship can take the form of offering food to the gods. It is then eaten by the worshippers and the priests, and must be vegetarian.

it is about equal to drinking intoxicating liquor. Ancient India's great epic, the Mahabharatha, raises the matter to a poetic level: 'Woman is an all-devouring curse,' it says. Noble man, it goes on to say, is unfortunately 'born out of lust engendered by blood and semen.' That the lust is shared by the man, and the semen is by definition his sole responsibility, is a fact sweepingly ignored in the writer's fury. He goes on, 'Man emerges mixed with excrement and water, fouled with the impurities of woman. A wise man will avoid the contaminating society of woman as he would the touch of bodies infested with vermin.'

Much of this sort of thing can be dismissed as Bible-thumpings, of which the West has had its share. But much reminds one of the sort of mental illnesses suffered by men who compulsively wash their hands twenty times a day.

Brahmins were, indeed, fanatically attached to being clean. They bathed scrupulously every day, often more than once. Pollution, with which we are so concerned in these times, was really an invention of the Hindu's, centuries ago. Their type of pollution came from contact with a lower caste, even from eating out of a vessel he had used. Thus, women being of the lowest caste simply by being women, it was logical that to touch them meant pollution. It was awkward

< *An elderly Hindu woman going to a cave by the sea for private prayers.*

(Overleaf) The Hindu gods Saraswati, Ganesh and Laxmi. Note the typical backcloth.

27

A young Brahmin.

A Hindu shrine on the beach, like the one on page 23.

that a Brahmin had to be procreated by another Brahmin. Brahmins claimed many miraculous powers, but none, so far as I know, ever claimed that little Brahmins could be born in a bottle. It had to be done in the traditional – and disgusting – way. This difficulty was got round by the invention of elaborate de-pollution ceremonies, and a good deal of puritanical breast-beating.

At this point I should make clear that I have been describing a historical situation, not the state of affairs in contemporary India. Today Brahmins mix freely with all other classes: outcastes sit cheek by jowl with them in the councils that guide the nation. Men and women are equal before the law. And as for the act of conception in the body of a woman, it is no longer considered polluting, though some Indians, who are concerned with the country's growing population problems, nostalgically wish that it were.

Yet something remains. In no other country is chastity so admired. Mahatma Gandhi preached and practised it. Whereas, in the West, the decline in the sexual powers is regretted in an aging male, in India the change is welcomed as a good riddance. As we shall see, the sages of the Upanishads did not disapprove of sex at the right age, nor did they think a woman was polluting, but they did say that a man loses something of himself in the sexual act, and many a thoughtful man would agree with them.

But I have travelled far from the age of Brahmin totalitarianism and it is time to return.

The rebels

To a Western reader, the system I have described will seem strange and even monstrous. That is because we have been brought up to believe that every man and woman wants liberty. But that is not true. Liberty of speech means very little to someone who has nothing to say: liberty of thought has no attractions for a man whose mind is a constant blank: liberty of movement does not concern a woman who thinks there is no place like home. It is obvious, moreover, that the vast majority of men and women have no objection to being told what to do with their sexual organs; otherwise morality would not have been so popular down the centuries.

While a contemporary Hindu can see the faults in the caste system, he is often inclined to say in its defence that it worked very well for a long time. In fact, the broad mass of the people did not object to the Brahmin hegemony until the West broke into the tranquil land. The West accused the Hindus of being static and hostile to change. But if they were against change, does it not mean they were happy?

Most of them were: but, almost from the beginning, a minority was not; it was a minority that included some of the most remarkable men in the history of India. They were rebels, and their theories can still make easy-going people decidedly uncomfortable. Perhaps that is why their names are rarely heard. The present-day swamis and gurus do not mention them in the peaceful precincts of their ashrams. But if these rebels had not existed, the gurus would not be there. It was the rebels who laid the foundations of the Upanishads.

Brihaspati was one of them. He lived sometime between 500 BC and AD 500 or so we guess: we know nothing personally about him, which is a pity, for he would be as interesting a man to meet as Voltaire. The two have a great deal in common.

He was such an upsetting man to the orthodox that none of his works have survived. Fortunately, he was so irritating that the orthodox itched to refute him, in case he should corrupt the faithful. But to do that, they had to quote him, and it is from these fragments that we get some glimpses of what he taught.

The Vedas were (and still are) revered as sacred and God-sent. Brihaspati said they were claptrap, cooked up by a bunch of rogues. The Brahmins he described as lazy and soft-bellied. He raised the immemorial cry against the priesthood, namely, that they had found an easy way of living off the fat of the land without doing any work. The faithful paid them lavishly to make certain desirable things come about. When they did, the priests took the credit: when they didn't, the priests blamed it on the sins of the faithful, and asked for still more money to absolve them. He was astonished that people could be so stupid as to let their lives be governed by a book of verses (the Vedas) and predicted that no good could come of it. The Brahmins replied that he was obviously the work of the Devil (or, rather, devils, since Hinduism developed a whole host of them).

Another critic, Charvaka, was just as cutting about the Brahmins, but in addition was a profound philosopher. He dismissed all 'spiritual' ideas, including God, as improbable vapourings. The only real thing was matter. Like the modern behaviourists, he taught that mind itself was matter and that everything we know comes from the perceptions of our five senses. The Scottish philosopher Hume demonstrated that nobody could really prove that something happened *because* something else had happened before, and this disturbing thought has never been refuted. Charvaka maintained the same thing: there was no such thing as cause and effect. Hume, having proved his point, remarked that he personally was not going to let it alter his own life by a jot: it was all a philosophical game. With Charvaka, it was more serious. If there was no cause and effect, then the claims of the priests to be able to make things happen were false and not to be believed. What did make things happen was a sort of destiny in everything, some special way of arranging matters.

Fortified by his theory, he attacked religion with even more venom than Brihaspati. The Brahmins had said that a man should look upon touching a woman as though he were touching a body with vermin. The vermin, said Charvaka, were the priests themselves. He denounced all religious practices whatever, from rites to pilgrimages, holding that they were only inventions to make money for the Brahmins.

Brihaspati may have been a voice crying in the wilderness. Charvaka was not. His ideas were so attractive that he gathered others around him who founded a whole school of philosophy.

The Nastika School, as it was called (the name means nay-sayers), were inevitably faced with the question, 'If it is stupid to do what the Brahmins say we should do, then what *should* we do?' The question was awkward: if the Nastikas gave detailed advice they would be coming dangerously close to those 'scorpions', as they called the Brahmins. One of them, Javali, came up with a tempting solution. Why try to be virtuous?, he asked. Is there really anything in this rigmarole of good advice which is dinned into our ears from childhood? Is it sensible to be filial and respect our mothers and fathers (since they are merely human beings, and often lamentably so)? Should a sensible man with eyes in his head honour his country, given what he could see that was going on it it? Wasn't morality just a trap set by the priests for us to fall into?

These sceptical questions have always been good ones. They seem to clear the mind. But they merely suggest what we should *not* do. Something positive was needed.

At this point, inspiration seems to have left them, Charvaka, Javali, and all the Nastikas. Their answer was eat, drink and be merry, for tomorrow you die, and there is nothing beyond that.

It would not serve. It never has served. It all seems so blunt and sensible at first glance, but it always leaves the feeling that the issue has been dodged. There is something more than hedonism. Given that priests are preposterous, that religion is nonsense, that obedience to the commands of God a foolishness because he does not exist, there still is a feeling that something has been ignored: there is something to be discovered.

That, at much the same time as the sceptical Nastikas, is what the sages of the Upanishads set out to do.

It is important to know the mood they were in when they set out because it is very like our own. We, too, are sceptics. We do not believe very much in the way of life that we are required to follow. Let us put aside those shallow people who indulge in the easy rhetoric that living in a highly organized society is a lonely, uncomfortable, and 'alienating' experience. It plainly is not. Never have human beings been so warm, cool, healthy and generally comfortable as they can make themselves in a modern city. Never have they had such an easy means of com-municating with their fellow men if they want to. Bringing people together has become a profession. In any Western country, as well as Russia or China, a hermit would have to be extremely dogged to maintain his stance. Are there any left? Outside India I have never heard of them.

Our scepticism comes from a deeper source. We listen to the prophets of doom but we notice that they drum up meetings to hear them. We read the moanings of the alienated but we notice that they use the means of communication – the press, television and books – with enviable expertise. De Gaulle was correct in saying that Jean-Paul Sartre was one of the glories of France: but the philosopher of the meaninglessness of living did not achieve that status by turning his back on life. He thoroughly enjoys being among people, provided, of course, they are his sort of people.

No. It is not this fashionable malaise that concerns us. Our concern is *us*. I shall not enlarge upon that last sentence at the moment: I shall leave it to the sages of the Upanishads.

They were a strange lot, and the strangest thing about them is that they have influenced the world down to this day without making any effort to do so. There is something profoundly moving in the thought of Jesus of Nazareth treading the hot roads of Galilee, preaching to all who would hear him, burning with his message. The Upanishadic sages went nowhere. They sat down in some delectable spot, built a hut, and stayed there. Had they not had disciples, we would not even know what they taught. But the disciples came, endured a series of polished insults, and left with strict instructions not to spread the teaching. The word 'Upanishad' itself means something to be kept secret, and the sages stressed that it should be kept especially secret from fools.

In short, they were crotchety. This has led earnest students of their teachings to try to make them into bearded, grandfatherly figures, exuding sweetness and light. They make them into persons as attractive as Gautama Buddha. They were not, and the difference is vital.

Everybody knows that Gautama Buddha was at first Prince Siddharta. He must have lived at much the same time as the sages of the Upanishads, though no precise date can be given to either. Living in luxury, he saw, on successive days, an old man, a sick man, and a corpse. It struck him (as it has struck much lesser observers) that life was a sad and random affair, guaranteeing nothing but an unhappy ending.

Now if any person nowadays should start thinking in the manner of the Buddha, society has a host of ways of quietening him. He can help heal the sick: he can alleviate the miseries of the old: and there is religion to console him about death. In much the same way, Siddharta had the Brahmins to hand. They would agree that life was a sorry business. They would make it an even more miserable affair by telling him that mortals had more than one life: they were reborn and they expiated the sins of the previous life in the new one: if they were fairly bad, their new life would be fairly miserable: if they were very bad, they could even be reborn as an animal. If they were good – exceptionally good – they could be reborn in that haven of blessedness, the household of a Brahmin. They could not, be it noted, be born a Brahmin.

If Siddharta had asked what he would have to do to be given this privilege, the Brahmins would have willingly told him. Principally, he should believe without a tremor of doubt in the Vedas, and therefore, give generously to the Brahmins. He could look all about his father's kingdom and find people living contentedly as was possible in this vale of tears, by following this advice.

We have seen that this is possible: people are not as attached to freedom as we would like to believe. But it would seem that even then there were some un-named eccentrics who did not toe the line. These followed a cult which existed long before the Aryans came to India, and which we will find still flourishing in our own twentieth century.

This taught that if a man practised austerities for several years – starving himself to the limit of endurance, sitting in one posture, controlling his breathing, retaining his semen in his body – he would win exceptional powers. He, as well as the Brahmins, could magically influence the course of things, and without reference to any gods there might, or might not, be.

Siddharta joined these. After torturing his body and bowels for some years in this manner, he found it got him no nearer the explanation of life. It should also be noted that he did not claim it had given him any special powers.

He then resorted to quiet, comfortable meditation, sitting under a tree. He emerged from this with the doctrine that if a certain way of life was followed it would end with a release from bodily existence: one would pass into Nirvana. This teaching immediately attracted followers but, regrettably, they did not write it down until two hundred years after the Buddha's death. Buddhism subsequently split into several sects, each of which had its own idea of what Nirvana was. It would be rash for any objective observer to say which of these accurately reflected the original teaching, or if any of them did.

Nor does it concern us here. What is important to our purpose is that the Buddha came back into the world. He clearly did not think much of it (or of the Brahmins), for he taught his followers that they should form communities of their own. In their monasteries they should follow eight rules of conduct which so closely resemble the higher moral teachings of Jesus of Nazareth that they have always had great appeal to the Western world.

But he did not say that these rules could be fully practised *in* the world. To do so, one must withdraw from it. He, then, was the first of the rebels who had an answer.

The next were the sages of the Upanishads.

Emperor Asoka, shaded by a ceremonial umbrella, pays homage to the Buddha, who is here represented by the Bodhi tree. (Relief on the north gate of the great stupa, Sanchi; photo Martin Hürlimann.)

A chela, or pupil, is studying under a guru. According to the Upanishads, wisdom can only be acquired by attending a sage.

How the Upanishads began

The Brahmins, who arranged everything, inevitably fixed the stages of a man's life. There were four of them, excluding childhood. The first stage was that of a schoolboy. He had to study under some teacher, who would instruct him in the Vedas. He was not supposed to have sex with women: if he did, he had to go around dressed in the skin of an ass for seven days. His education took twelve years.

He then passed to the stage of being a householder, a married man, and the father of a family. During this period, he was required to be eminently respectable, obeying the rules laid down in his education, being a good citizen, a good father, and finally a good grandfather.

When he could look down on the head of his son's son (as the texts put it) he had to retire. Pleasant places in the forest were appointed for this, where he could live with other retired people. This, because it represented a stage in a man's life, was called a 'staging place' or ashram.

The majority of men who went to the ashram must have died there, since the expectation of life was shorter than it is today. But those who attained a ripe old age could pass to the fourth and last stage, in which the old man gave up all his worldly goods and, taking a robe, a staff and a begging bowl, lived the life of a holy mendicant. This entailed a good deal of discomfort, but it earned him the reverence of the young.

It will be noticed how all this resembles our own social organization. We have the same divisions – school, raising a family, and retirement to such places as Florida, the Riviera, or Bournemouth. We do not have the begging bowl period, although many of the aged living on a state pension might consider it not a bad idea. Instead of the open road we have our Old Folks' Homes, which prevent the ancients from impeding the traffic.

Now the intention of the Brahmins was that the boy should be taught the Vedas, the householder practise them (with the aid of the priests) and the retired man study them. The sages of the Upanishads made a bold change in the programme. They retired to the ashrams, but instead of thinking exclusively about the Vedas, they thought about themselves. For the rest of this book I shall be dealing with the revolutionary result of their thinking, but it is so startling and, to some, upsetting, that it is best to start with something familiar and close to hand.

In ancient India, women were not expected to follow the four stages. But in our world they do. Let us take an average woman in the West: let us make her neither very poor nor very rich, so that she will have an even tenor to her life, so far as material things go. Let us see what happens to her.

Her parents will tell her what society expects of her: school will equip her with the education necessary for her to play her part in it. She will have a whole set of ideas in her head, none of which is her own. As she grows into young womanhood she may have a period when she does some thinking for herself, which will lead her to demonstrations, marches and the like. This will arouse dismay among her parents and other elders, and will seem important to herself: that is, until something overwhelmingly more important happens to her – she falls in love.

At home and at school she was not her own mistress: others guided and dominated her life. She may have resented this: but now that she is in love she is even more dominated, and she would not have it otherwise. Indeed, she would be desperate if it were. She dresses, talks, eats and drinks to please and attract her lover. She is ecstatic when she finds that his thoughts and opinions are her thoughts and opinions, and when they are not she strives to put herself right. Her hours are not her own, they are his. An embrace and a kiss from him, the whole world is a happy, roseate place: a sudden coldness from him, and the whole world grows chill. When they are happy together, her thoughts are all of him; when they quarrel, it is still worse: he becomes an obsession until the quarrel is made up.

She is now so much in love that she decides to share her life with him. They get married. Let us not be cynical, but let us grant her at least a few years of happiness. But let us also take note that a thing shared is not wholly your own. The marriage proceeds: her husband may be far from taking the view of women that the law-maker Manu did. He may be ready to give her any liberty she asks for. But she does not want him to give her too much. She likes to feel free, but she likes much more to be needed. Well, then, let us say, he needs her, she lovingly meets his needs, and since having one's needs met is very attractive, he needs her more and more. They have children. She feels fulfilled. But as the months and years roll by, the children remind her by wails, shrieks, tantrums, mischief and endless battles that they are very far from fulfilled themselves. The husband, hitherto blissfully accumulating his needs, finds one day that his needs cause hysterics and things to be thrown at his head.

Her children grow up. Her husband loses his hair and his charm; his charm, that is, for her, but unfortunately not for certain other women. Her husband is as much in her mind as he was before they were married.

Then something happens that makes her take a long look at her life – the death of her parents, an illness, a tour to strange lands alone. Let us be generous and give her three weeks in a Caribbean paradise. In this paradise she meets a loquacious Snake, the sort of man who specializes in understanding women who are approaching middle age. She listens to him. One night (let it be still and starry) she realizes that she has never led a life of her own. Schoolteachers, parents, lover-boy, Daddy, the kids, they all ran her life for her. It was plainly a state of affairs which could satisfy nobody, except perhaps lawgiver Manu, who would have told her that, being a woman, she deserved no more.

We may wind up her story, for there is little more to tell. She parts from the Serpent, who, while she cries on his shoulder, tells her to remember the words of Socrates, 'To thine own self be true.' This is no use at all. It was not Socrates who said them but Shakespeare, and she cannot be true to herself because, as she now realizes, she has no idea who her own-self is: nor is she ever likely to find out.

With that last observation we take our first step along the path traced out by the sages of the Upanishads. I have been along it to the end and I can confirm that it is, at times, a dangerous path for the unwary. The Upanishads, in a rather exaggerated metaphor, call it the 'razor's edge'. It may not be as narrow as that, but you can certainly slip off it.

The sages are mostly mere names to us, except for one. He is Yajnavalkya. We meet him when he is already an old man. It is clear that he was contentious, very clever in argument, and highly sceptical, particularly of the Brahmins and their sacrifices. Perhaps because he wanted to get away from their dragooning, perhaps because he was prepared to make one last act of conformity, he decided to retire to the forest as was prescribed for those of his age.

This withdrawal entailed the giving away of his property – in fact, the whole routine may have been devised to make sure an old man did not hang on to his wealth too long. Yajnavalkya had two wives, and we have vivid pictures of them. One likes fine clothes, jewellery, chariots and the good life. The other is more thoughtful. The first wife gets her share and is quite content, the second has doubts. She asks her husband if money and goods would make her immortal. Yajnavalkya tells her that it won't. She then presses him to tell her what would do so. It is clear that in asking to be 'immortal' she is merely using a word out of her limited vocabulary to eradicate a suspicion that has grown in her mind. She feels that her husband has some secret of the greatest importance which he will not willingly divulge to two mere wives. Therefore she renounces her share of the family property, provided she can follow her husband into the forest and there learn the truth about things. He agrees. She goes with him to the forest, and he initiates her into the secret teaching.

Now it is clear that there were other sages much in Yajnavalkya's state of mind about the regimented world that they lived in. It is also certain that there were other women who followed them into the forest. One of them has, in fact, earned immortality: she plagues the philosopher with such persistence that he finally roars at her, 'Do not ask too many questions, woman, or your head will fall off.'

The questions that both the women and the men of the time were asking (when, that is, they had not been brainwashed) were the commonest queries of all: who am I? How did I come here? Where am I going? Is there a God? If so, who is he? The dazzling achievement of the Upanishadic sages is that by concentrating on the first of these questions they answered the last.

The teaching that Yajnavalkya gave to his wife was the same as that of all the other sages of the Upanishads. They invite you to sit down quietly and think about yourself. You should do it with as little distraction as possible, either from people or such simple things as indigestion. It is unfortunate that this process has come to be called 'meditation'. That word has a most unfortunate connotation for most of us in the West. It conjures up visions of monks with their hands in the sleeves of their habits walking peacefully in cloisters, silent save for the hum of bees, or of clear-complexioned nuns on faldstools, meditating to the sound of an organ. The 'meditation' of the Upanishads has nothing to do with that, and it might be more popular if it had. It is merely hard, plain thinking, until you arrive at the end of the journey. Nor has it got anything to do with sitting in odd postures. (I shall explain the place of Yoga later.) You can, in fact, do *anything* you like, provided you think. We all know a thousand ways to avoid doing that: these must be abandoned, of course. But we may get our brain to work in which-ever way suits us best.

The subject of our thoughts must be ourselves. This sounds a most agreeable thing to do, and there is the first place where it is easy to slip off the path. When we think of ourselves, we must not approve (which is easy enough) nor dis-approve. We must not aim to make ourselves better nor regret our shortcomings. When anyone brought up in a Jewish or Christian environment attempts this, he or she will discover, with a sense of shock, how much religion has moulded the mind. To study the simplest past situation involving yourself in a completely objective way may take weeks of daily thinking before you succeed.

But with practice you can succeed. Many attempts have been made to describe this process by some parallel experience. I think each person had best make his own, but for me it is much like being in a theatre. At first you are on the stage, and you are the principal actor in the drama, which is about your life. There are others in the plot, but you take notice of them only when they come in on cue. This is much what we all do in a normal reverie. But provided you are not interrupted in your thinking, provided you do not play too much to the gallery, you grow tired of acting the role, much as an actor gets tired of his most successful part when the run is very long. (That is important: you should go over and over and over a scene till you are bored.) You call your understudy, and step down into the auditorium to watch him. He is so good he might be yourself: but *you* are now in the stalls.

To change the illustration for a moment. Many people have had the experience of finding themselves portrayed in a novel written by a friend. I myself am a predatory writer in this respect: those who have been my victims have told me that it has been an amused, detached, experience. Just so, in the silence of your room, in a seat in that imaginary theatre, you grow detached – or you should do. If you leap from your seat in disgust or anger or in delight at yourself, and you do that too many times, you should give the whole thing up. It is the first slip from the path, but it can be fatal to your peace of mind to continue the journey.

If you do not slip, there is considerable entertainment in it for you. As well as being the principal actor, and the spectator, you are also the playwright. It is, after all, your own life you are watching.

Or *are* you the playwright? More and more it seems to you that it is the other characters who are building the plot, dictating your movements, inventing your lines for you to speak. You have much the same experience as that poor woman whom we sent to the Caribbean, and saw her life for what it was on that still and starlit night.

Yet if we sit very still, very watchful, thinking, we do not feel the need to cry on anyone's shoulder. We sit absorbed; the plot is most ingenious: all those people – relatives, friends, instructors, priests, politicians, conspiring so cleverly to make something you have thoughtlessly called *me* for so long.

Now order the curtain to be rung down. Leave the theatre, in other words, leave the room in which you have been thinking and go out into the world for a while. Shake hands, smile, eat, drink, be merry or sad. Something of that detachment will remain with you. Just as, on leaving an absorbing play, you cannot quite focus the street outside, the rain, the taxis and the cars, so there is a touch of unreality about the world outside your room. There is also a touch of unreality about you, that other you that has been on the stage. You can, in glimpses, observe him shaking hands, smiling, being merry or sad. Poor fellow, little does he know who made him. You do, at least in part.

I trust I am not making things sound too humourless, because at this stage there is a good deal of comedy. All young people have met the exasperating old man who will not take good advice; not from them, not from anybody. He is exasperating because the advice is meant only for his own good – his health, his affairs, his future such as he has left. He greets it all with a superior smile – or cackle – and a shake of his head.

When you have examined things and found out how little you can claim to be really yourself, you are in something of the state of mind of that old man. Imagine your real self, untouched by the influences of others: a blank white wall, shall we say. As the years of infancy, childhood and youth pass, innumerable people scribble on it, some writing their own names, others slogans. Others write abuse, others their favourite obscenities. In the end there is nothing of the white wall left, only a mass of graffiti, one upon the other, scribbles on scribbles done by alien hands.

The sages of the Upanishads invite you to stand back and survey this wall. Should you do it, it is comic to observe some new person advance upon it with the desire to leave his mark upon the others. There are those who are anxious to tell us, unasked, what to do, what to think, how to make love – the wiseacres, the moralists, the politicians. For the sages, it was the priests. They regarded them with a smile, and taught their disciples to do the same.

We can now pass to the next step. The method is the same. We sit quietly thinking in our hut in the forest, or our silent room, and we go on thinking about ourselves: we continue to ask 'Who am I?'

We might think that the next thing to do was to wash the wall and free it from the graffiti. Then we would be our true selves again. But the sages were not optimists. They say that it cannot be done. It is a key point to understand, and it is very Indian. Throughout Hindu history, from before the Brahmins down to this very moment, it has always been believed that what we do stays with us and what is done stays too. Our life is a lengthening chain which we drag with us, and we cannot lose a link of it. There is no sense of salvation; there is no way of being washed whiter than the snow. The Brahmins, of course, said that in a limited way there was. By paying them to say the right spells, one could be relieved of some of the burden. But even they preached that reincarnation in a series of new lives was necessary for a final absolution.

The sages of the Upanishads dismissed this view as priestly trickery. Instead they substituted a doctrine of their own. It was profoundly original: it has no parallel anywhere else in the history of thought, and it is the heart of their teaching.

The still centre

We must abandon the metaphor of the wall, which was my own, and take up that of the sages themselves.

We have examined the various stages of our lives. None of them can we call our true selves. Others made them. Consider then, say the sages, all our life as an onion. The various phases of our lives are the leaves. Since we are looking for our true selves, pure and uncontaminated, we must throw away each of the layers. But if you do this with a real onion, when finally you brush away the tears, you will find yourself with one leaf between your fingers. This, too, must be thrown away. Then you have nothing – nothing at all.

'Excellent!' say the sages. 'That is the answer.'

It is an answer which has astonished people, dismayed them, and repelled them for two thousand years. Yet in all those centuries there have always been enquirers whom it has fascinated. They have returned to it, puzzled over it, and finally understood it. They have always been a minority, as the sages said they would be.

Before we join the minority, let us stand for a moment on more familiar ground. We have seen that the Indian sceptics, such as Javali, had said that if one looked closely into the matter, all instructions, advice, theories and such about the right way to live were nonsense, the biggest nonsense of all being religion. The gods of the altars did not exist, their commands were forgeries made by the priests. The best, the only sensible thing to do was to enjoy life to the full while it lasted. Your own happiness was all that counted, with no incidental claptrap about the greatest happiness of the greatest number. There are no moral or social duties except to avoid exasperating your neighbour to the point where he gets you slammed into jail.

But in order to know what makes you happy, you must know yourself. So we have taken a step upwards from the mundane level of the hedonists – but we have stepped on thin air. We hastily step backwards and downwards.

< *This picture has been chosen by a learned swami as symbolic of the process by which aspects of the personality are stripped away one by one, until the spirit is freed (see the bird).*

To anybody brought up in the West, an escape suggests itself. It is part of the Christian ethic that a man must lose his soul in order to gain it. At first sight it seems that this is what we have been doing while we followed the sages. We breathe easily again, for a while.

However, it does not bear examination. What Jesus taught is very clear. By losing our souls (or selves) he meant that we should rid ourselves of our selfishness, our pride, our egotism. We do this by following his precepts, laid down forever in the Sermon on the Mount. We should forgive others, help the unfortunate, be kind to them, be humble in doing good, and ask forgiveness for our own sins. Surely this is a better answer to our question 'Who am I?' than the one provided by hair- (or rather onion-) splitting Orientals? Who am I? Nothing very much, it seems, may the Lord forgive me.

I am not denying that, for those who wish it, it may be a better answer. But it is nothing to do with the Upanishads, as I can testify on high authority.

For many years I lived in Rome and had much to do with the Vatican in pursuit of my profession as a writer. I often spoke with the prelates there of such things as the Upanishads and the Bhagavad Gita and I had the honour of their sometimes consulting me. There is a large Catholic population in India, eight million or so, and Indians are trained as priests to serve this community. The brightest of these seminarists are carried to Rome to complete their studies. This includes a great deal of learning about Catholic theology, the philosophy, that is, of the faith.

Every so often, one of these Indian students, carried away by his studies, turns to the philosophers of his native land. He takes up the Upanishads and, like so many other people of developed intelligence, he is bowled over by them. The monseigneurs of the Vatican describe it sharply as 'another Indian gone bonkers'.

The Indian seminarist, teetering between two faiths, invariably tries to combine the two. They are, he argues, saying the same thing. To this the Rector who is directing his studies replies in no uncertain terms that they are not. The Catholic faith is what they have been trying to drive into his head over the last few years: the Upanishads are amoral and godless, in the sense that they are without a personal god. Meantime the monseigneurs shake their heads and say, 'A brilliant boy, but he'll never make a bishop.' If the Indian does not withdraw his arguments, he is unlikely to get even a parish.

The Vatican is right: it can serve as a warning as we proceed in this inquiry. We shall find a number of well-meaning and good-hearted people who say that all religions are really the same. In fact, this has become a cliché among people who have no religion at all, and do not care to have. To me it is a doubtful argument. It is like saying that violet, indigo, blue, green, yellow, orange and red are really all the same colour because when you blend them together they make white. This view has a special appeal to educated Christians because Christianity, as we know it today, is in fact a blending of faiths, many of them dating from classical times. It is, in the words of Norman Douglas, 'an Alexandrian *tutti-frutti*'.

But the teachings of the Upanishads cannot be blended. An attempt to do so resulted in one of the most sublime poems ever written, the Bhagavad Gita. For all the skill of the poet, they still emerge pristine and unaltered. They are not a religion. A religion must have a god, or gods. It must have ceremonies of worship: it must have a clear moral code. The Upanishads have none of those. They stand out in the history of human thought as unique, a Taj Mahal in speculation.

The discovery that the thinkers of the Upanishads made is simple to describe but difficult to practise. You have, let us assume, analyzed your life down to the last skin of the onion. You have discarded this, and you are left with nothing. You have been searching for your true self, but you have found that everything about you has been produced by others. The next step needs some preparation. This can be various but I shall take the exercise of Bhagwan Shree Rajneesh, a contemporary swami.

He tells you to take a flower. There is no significance in its being a flower. It can be anything – a parcel, a ring, or even your spouse. Now, adopting any position in which you feel comfortable, look at the flower. Think about it, but with your true self, that *nothing* you found in the onion.

Do not, says Rajneesh, think of it as beautiful. That is something you have been taught by others. Do not think of it as a botanical specimen. Botany is not a subject you have invented by yourself. If it is a rose, for instance, do not think of all the associations you have with a rose: they come from your past. If you are of a literary bent, do not even say 'A rose is a rose is a rose'. That appears to be near what Rajneesh is after, but it will be found that it is not. Gertrude Stein has used *words*. You must abandon words. Words were what you learned at your mother's knee, and your mother's knee is the last thing we want butting into our experiment.

In ten minutes, you will give up exhausted. Thinking nothing is intensely difficult, in spite of the fact that we all know people who seem to do nothing else the livelong day. It would probably occur to you that it would be better to take something that has no meaning for you – a point of light, for example. It is worth trying because it gives you some encouragement: for a minute or so you do feel that your mind is blank. Unfortunately, it will not remain so for long.

49

(Overleaf) Meditation: here a man uses the glittering sea to fix his mind.

Thoughts and images will come creeping back, stealing upon you unawares. Then you will merely be in a reverie: that is quite a pleasant state, but it no more concerns what you are trying to do than lying on a beach in the sun and dreaming.

It is now imperative to leave the experiment. To strain the mind to stop thinking can result in something as unspiritual as a bad headache. You should relax, go about your business, and, in spare moments, try to find out where you have gone wrong. Contrast any fifteen minutes of the day with what you felt looking at the rose. You will see that in your normal life you are constantly making judgments, from whether to put another spoonful of sugar in your coffee or whether to start proceedings for divorce.

Now your judgments cannot be the real you for they all come from the society in which you live and in which you have been reared. It is comparatively easy to stop making them for a few moments: the sugar is white crystals and you need not worry, for once, whether it will add to your waistline. Your husband is *there*, a male body, and you need not worry, temporarily, about whose bed he puts it in when your back is turned. Some people have a knack of doing this. The Italian author Guareschi had a way with letters: he put them, unopened, on an armchair in an empty room, which he proudly showed to his publisher, his agent and other visiting correspondents. It will be seen that letters are something which Guareschi made no judgment about.

That last example will have made you uneasy. You hope that to pursue your study of the Upanishads, you will not be asked to throw away your letters, because that would be alarming. It is precisely that state of alarm which is the beginning of wisdom. The sages of the Upanishads are extremely alarming, so much so that strenuous attempts were made for centuries to camouflage what they were saying. But it is quite clear. They are saying that your real self cannot possibly care a rap for other people, or society, or success, or failure, or laws, or morals. Your various false selves can rollick in all these things: your real self, pure and undefiled by others, is supremely indifferent to them. It is a revolutionary teaching: and to a person who values being respectable, it can be very upsetting.

After that warning you may feel it would be safer with the Brahmins and their meticulously ordered world. On the other hand, you may feel like the sages, and find the pressures of an organized world intolerable. In that case, you will continue. That can best be done by practising non-judging for a brief period every day. It is worth doing: it is useful. Guareschi would joke that, in due course, most letters answer themselves. If someone writes to ask what an author's next book will be about, the correspondent will, after all, be fully answered when he sees it on the bookstall.

In much the same way, if you suspend judgment about, shall we say, some quarrel you are having, when you return to judging, the quarrel often seems much less important. Suppose there is a person you are normally quite sure is a scoundrel: if you can stop being worked up about the villain for a little while, you may, when you return to judging, find that there is some good in him after all. A wise High Court Judge that I once knew made it a practice never to think about the cases before him once under his own roof.

By the constant practice of non-judging, you withdraw, step by step, from the snares and anxieties of daily life, just as the sages withdrew from the towns and the Brahmins as they walked into the forest. You may now return to your rose.

You will find it much easier to still the tumult of your mind: it will be simple to suspend judgment of the rose. But you must also still the activity of your body. I do not mean you should stop your breathing, stand on your head, or eat nothing but uncooked vegetables. You should, however, choose a time for your non-thinking in which you are neither replete with food nor hungry for the next meal. Your posture should be the most comfortable one you know, with your muscles relaxed. To an observer (but do not allow observers) you should look like a thoroughly idle person with the expression of the village idiot chewing a straw. If we could ever observe what goes on in a village idiot's mind, I would not be surprised to learn that it frequently approaches transcendental meditation.

It may take months, or even years, but one day you will arrive at a point when you have nothing to say about the rose, but that you are *aware* of it. This neutral awareness is a singular thing. It is much sharper than a normal impression, though it has nothing of the hallucinatory about it. You cannot really see a person's face as it is if you are in love with him or her, or if you are angry. But you often have a sharp impression of a face you have seen in the street, knowing nothing about its owner and caring nothing. In the same way, viewing things about you with a tranquil, non-judging eye, in total calm, not curious about whence things came, nor where they are going, feeling no emotion of any sort, then you see not as in a glass darkly, but face to face.

This tranquil eye is your true self. You have found it imperceptibly. It has been done in such small stages, you are unaware of how far you have come. Your true self feels no joy. You have none of the ecstasy of the mystic Christian with his visions of ineffable glory. You are not filled with the love of God. There is no God. It is a little like being peacefully asleep while extremely wide awake. But, I must repeat, there is no God.

Perhaps the greatest disservice to Indian thought was done by Aldous Huxley. He was a man of unusual mental powers and very proud of having them. Brought up in a Western culture – cultured, indeed, to exasperation – he applied his intellect to the Upanishads and found what he was looking for. He hated India, and so was greatly relieved to find that the mystics of the Upanishads were much the same as Christian mystics. An anthology of quotations taken out of context seemed to prove his point. Other intelligent people, anxious to avoid the unsettling doctrines of the sages, eagerly drank in the bland mixture that Huxley had brewed for them. We must now put all that aside, and check on what the sages really said at the very core of their teaching.

Brahma and the atom

I do not know whether the reader shares my feelings, but when I find myself at a point when a book (or a swami) promises me the ultimate revelation, I grow suspicious. So many times it ends up in rhetoric, of the sticky sweet-tasting variety, reminding me of my definition of perfect contentment when I was a small boy – a room filled with chocolate cream bars, with just enough room for me. We can all cope with the religious enthusiast who exudes an air of 'holier than thou'. He may be, and good luck to him. But present-day expounders of the Upanishads often assume an air of 'wiser than thou' which I find impertinent, especially when I catch them out on the next page (or during the next minute) in some howling historical error. Swamis and gurus should, I think, avoid quoting Western history: they are busy men and history is a tricky subject.

In particular, I always prick up my ears when I hear the word 'universe'. If I am told that at the end of the transcendental jaunt I shall feel myself at one with this very large object, I fasten my seat-belt and check what I already know about it. After all, the universe puzzled Einstein to the end of his life.

In the classical age of Greece, the philosopher Democritus, merely by thinking about it, decided it was made of atoms. This theory, at the time, was considered interesting but far-fetched. With the fall of Greece and its successor, Rome, it was replaced, after a considerable interval, by the theory that the universe was the creation of a beneficent God the Father, out of love for mankind. This was even more far-fetched, but it held sway. It taught that all was right with the world, even if you could scarcely wake up any morning of the week without finding that everything was wrong with it.

There were some doubters who felt that the universe was not quite fully explained by this theory. But after the Church burned a few of these trouble-makers at the stake things settled down. The swamis and gurus of the time (I mean Popes and priests) hit upon the argument that the only way to understand the orthodox theory of the universe was just to swallow it hook, line and sinker, and keep it down as best you may. The curious have only to turn to the impressive writings of St Thomas Aquinas (which begin with this reasoning) to find out how convincing it is.

In the seventeenth, eighteenth, and above all in the nineteenth century, some men, with much troubling of their spirits, began to look at this beneficent gift of the Almighty, with instruments which grew increasingly refined. They found the universe was made of atoms. An Australian physicist put this beyond any doubt by sending a powerful current through some atoms in a Cambridge laboratory, and splitting them. I remember being taken as a schoolboy to meet this man, Lord Rutherford, and he showed me round his fantastic apparatus. I had been taken by some Indian friends of my family who felt my education needed modernizing. When I got back home, in response to my incessant questions, my Hindu father, who had dabbled in science, procured for me a piece of radio-active rock, which lit up the clock in my bedroom at night with a soft green glow.

They were innocent days. By good luck my blood was not poisoned, but my mind was changed. I remembered the rough charm of Rutherford as he explained what he was doing (truly great men are invariably courteous to enquiring boys); I pondered the green glow and imagined the bits of atoms it was shooting off, and I formed the conviction that these scientists would one day know what made the universe tick, just as I knew what made my bedroom clock do the same thing.

However, when I reached my late 'teens, I returned to the philosophers, for that, it was clear, was my natural bent, and not science. Reading Bertrand Russell, I was much struck by his pointing out that the table on which he was writing was not really solid, but a concourse of atoms and electrons whirling about in spaces as vast, comparatively, as that which separated the planets. This led me to reflect that the philosopher leaning on it was also made up of spinning particles, and I wondered why he had not mentioned it, since it would be a more telling example than the table. But practising to think of myself as this buzzing and porous affair, I saw that for an English gentleman of Russell's generation, the illustration would have been undignified.

The years passed. The collection of vibrating atoms that made up Bertrand Russell sat down firmly in front of the London police to protest against other atoms being split in a bomb. Manners and customs had changed: the English gentleman had disappeared, and our bodies were no longer protected from the scientists. Enquirers of all races were searching into the atoms and combinations of atoms that made us what we are.

In the late 'fifties and in the 'sixties of the twentieth century, those men found that my picture of Russell and myself was not just a student's imagining. It was true in an extraordinary way, and a way that was extraordinarily grim. Combinations of atoms in curling chains conveyed everything that made us, in journeys that sent them slithering through the protoplasm of the cell, to hook up with others and then make us, Russell, or me, or you. Genes, which were storehouses of these fatal particles, could turn us out Apollos or hunchbacks, geniuses or fools.

Other chemicals, along with mysterious electrical impulses, could flash through the body to other chemical complexes waiting in the brain and cause Russell to write the *Principia Mathematica*, or me to write my laundry list.

For a time I was relieved by the thought that no one knew what caused the molecular changes in the genes that made one man differ from another. There was still room for mystery. Maybe there still is, for a while, but I do not think it will be for long.

I found on deeper study that there was one theory, not unfavoured by the biological chemists, that some changes may be caused by particles shot out of the sun, and perhaps the stars, and entering the human body. I determined to see these particles. I conducted a simple experiment in the window of my apartment in the historic centre of Rome.★

By inverting a glass jar over some dry ice, I produced a thin fog inside it. Every so often there would be a faint flash. This was the track of a particle that had come from the sun. I would then walk out among the ruins of the city, on the hill where once stood the palace of the Caesars, and I would wonder if it was some such particle striking a womb at random in the imperial city that produced at one time Augustus, at another Nero, Caligula and Commodus.

My thoughts turned back to the time when it was thought that we were the products of a beneficent Creator, who watched Creation with a beneficent eye. But what would that eye see? It would see a complicated dance of electrons, protons, neutrons and the string of other whirligigs of force that are being discovered yearly in the cyclotrons. All would move according to formulas. There would be a formula for one set of particles and forces. That formula would be me, until I died and became another.

Just as Democritus, by thinking, discovered the atom, so the sages of the Upanishads discovered that picture of the Self which I have just described. It was a fact of their own experience. When they had stripped away their worldly personalities and entered into that tranquil neutral Self, they found a sense of

★It is described in the Encyclopaedia Britannica under *Cosmic Rays*.

identity with everything around them. They found it difficult to describe. They found words for the peeling of the onion: 'not this', they said, repeatedly. You are looking for your true self; well, it is not this and this and this. But when it came to describing the true self as identical with everything in the universe, their vocabulary betrayed them. 'This', they explained, 'is that.' To the misty-minded, such a phrase can sound portentous, but when a clear-headed person examines it, he can see that it is something of a failure, a waving of the hands when one cannot find the words one wants.

Yet it cannot be denied that their experience was genuine. The scientists, as we have seen, can raise no objection: we are made of the same building blocks as everything else. We can easily accept the vocabulary of Democritus; we know about his atoms. But the phrases of the Upanishads are still strange to us.

This has happened to us before. When, in the early decades of the twentieth century, Freud brought forward his hypotheses, there was considerable doubt among the informed, and positive disgust among the uninformed. The notion of the unconscious seemed vague and sounded more like a literary invention than a hard fact. To the common man, the notion that he was driven by sexual urges, some perverted, seemed exaggerated and grubby. Things were not helped by Freud himself who very clearly stated that, although his researches were based on patients who were mentally sick, he could not guarantee a cure.

But he had aroused a world-wide curiosity. People began using psycho-analytic terms, many of them invented in the Master's despite by his pupils. 'Inferiority complex', 'castration fears', 'the Oedipus complex', 'phallic symbols', 'father-figure' joined the cocktail party vocabulary and were caught up into the babble of students. Misused and often misunderstood, they did, all the same, seem to refer to something which went on in the human being. Freud, who himself was as moral as Moses, gave rise to the permissive society.

In much the same way, the phrases in which the Upanishadic sages expressed their deepest thoughts, have echoed about in thoughtful men's minds. They do so more than ever today. In the free world, we are freer to think about ourselves than we ever have been. We can even face having irreligious thoughts without a tremor. And there the sages have something strong for us. 'If this is that', they say, 'God is you and you are God.'

At first the idea of being God is beguiling: on second thoughts it is the most terrible thing that could ever be wished on us. A cautious reader of this book might well decide that if it was going to lead him to thinking he was the Almighty, the best thing to do with it would be to bury it in the backyard. The matter clearly needs explanation.

The great god Brahma in his three forms: Destroyer (left head), Creator (centre head) and Preserver (right head). From the colossal statue in the Elephanta cave.

By the time of the Upanishads, the Vedic gods had begun to disappear and to be replaced by less earthy figures. These, in turn, coalesced in the minds of the Brahmins into one god, Brahma, who had created and sustained the world. But Brahma was in no sense the monotheistic God of Abraham, or Mohammed. He was altogether vaguer. It was not even clear if he personally interfered in the affairs of mankind. Other lesser gods grew up beside him to perform those duties, with one of whom, Krishna, we shall have something to do later.

The idea of Brahma was very philosophical. People do not like philosophers whom they suspect of making things more difficult than they are, for professional reasons. Now Brahma had created the universe. A simpler idea grew up, even among the Brahmins themselves, that he *was* the universe. This notion – pantheism – has always been popular among people who cannot help noticing that they have a more refined nature than the vulgar. Thus well-bred ladies feel that they can see God in a sunset, minor poets are constantly seeing God in flowers: otherwise sober people, taking a brisk walk on a Spring morning, do not encounter, like Buddha, the old, the sick and the dead, but feel God all around them.

People who have thought deeply about spiritual matters – the saints, the philosophers – have always treated pantheists with marked contempt. St Francis of Assisi had a genuine love for the beautiful things of creation. But when he sang about the sun and the moon, he did not call them God. He called them his brother and his sister, which is one of the reasons why, when he saw the reigning Pope, he got on famously with him. Pantheists are despised because the thoughtful observer, while seeing that Creation can be a pretty sight at times, thinks that on balance it is a bleak affair.

Like most other philosophers, the Upanishadic sages dismissed pantheism. They saw that it was, in reality, a return to the old Vedic worship of the powers of nature. They took the word, 'Brahma', and gave it an entirely new meaning. They argued that since, in the ultimate analysis, you could not distinguish your real self from the rest of Creation, then *you* were that Creation. You, as they put it, were Brahma.

Most importantly of all, they did not mean that when you found your true self you had an ecstatic union with God. This is Christian mysticism in its very essence, but it is not at all that of the Upanishads. They would have nothing to do with *twos* – you and God, you and nature, you and Brahma. There is only a single thing at the end of it all – you.

This is a very simple doctrine and it was that simplicity that got it into trouble. No sooner had it spread among the intelligent than a series of attempts were made to explain it away. Some of these attempts were dishonest, such as corrupting the texts: others were made by sincere people, some with powerful intellects, who quite saw the consequences of the Upanishadic teaching, and could not believe that sages could be so bold, so rash and so destructive.

Hindus performing private devotions. The woman in the photograph above is reading extracts from the Gita.

A pavement artist drawing a representation of Ganesh. >

(Overleaf) Top, figure of Ganesh from the shrine shown on pp. 28–9; below and opposite, figures of Sai Baba, the popular Moslem mystic. A photograph of the contemporary Satya Sai Baba, who claims to be the reincarnation of Sai Baba, can be seen hanging on the shrine at top left.

The Upanishads corrupted

The sages of the Upanishads would probably regret that I can write and you can read. They could do neither and showed no desire to acquire the accomplishment. They insisted that their teachings should be learned by word of mouth (the word 'Upanishad' also means 'sit close beside me') and should not be spread abroad. Buddha organized a whole army of evangelists and was a superb one himself. The sages made no move to spread their gospel. They knew it was for the few who would take the trouble (and had the time) to understand it.

I fancy they would have been considerably amused if they could sit in at a modern ashram. Here their words are expounded by the guru, one by one, having first been read aloud in a resonant and solemn voice, in Sanskrit.

To the sages it would be gibberish. They spoke Prakrit, like everyone around them. Prakrit was a popular vernacular, useful in the daily round, but scarcely a literary language and not in any way a philosophical one.

Sanskrit came later. It was invented to nail down the texts of the Vedas, hitherto transmitted by ear. It was made very precise, for it had to fix the endless regulations by which society was governed. A language is precise only when it has a rigid grammar: we owe the first grammar-book to the Hindus. Unfortunately this grammar was so difficult that Sanskrit never became a popular language. It was, and is, understood by the few. The title 'Pandit', made famous by Jawaharlal Nehru, originally meant a man who was versed in Sanskrit, and this was so rare that a Pandit was revered. Nehru inherited it from his father, who knew a great deal of Sanskrit: his son knew little or none, and in order to govern India had absolutely no need to.

By the time that the pandits came to putting the Vedas into Sanskrit, the sacred texts had acquired all sorts of appendices. Among them were the Upanishads, of which there were over a hundred. Some of these were of little importance, but there were thirteen which taught the doctrine of the Self, and these had so

< Three wandering sadhus.

impressed themselves on the Hindu imagination that they could not be dropped, even if what they taught was in direct contradiction to the Vedas themselves.

There were two methods of dealing with a situation like this. One was to translate them and then declare firmly that they were not sacred, not part of the required reading. This is what the Christians did when drawing up the Bible. They laid down the rule that some texts constituted the canon, and that others were apocryphal. The apocryphal texts include one describing how St Peter had a competition in magic with a conjuror called Simon Magus and how he won it. Another describes how St Thomas came to India and converted a large number of people. What leaps to the eye in reading the Apocrypha is how much more shallow they are than the canon. Expunging them from the holy text caused very little loss.

With the Upanishads, the situation was just the reverse. Passages in them often seemed more profound than the Vedas themselves. Despite the fact that the sages were against the Brahmins, those Brahmins could not expunge them; not, at least, from men's minds. If they had tried, something would be sure to linger. They have that effect even today. No matter how casually they are read, or how sceptically, there will be a passage which suddenly arrests your thoughts: a phrase will move you and will stay in your mind. An Indian writer has said that he once saw a page from the Upanishads blowing across a courtyard in the breeze. He read a fragment, and it changed his life. That is possibly a little romantic, but anyone who has read them will agree that something like this does happen.

The Sanskrit scholars therefore translated them and did not remove them from the canon. But they used the second method of dealing with the problem. They subtly changed them by using their own vocabulary. The effect can best be understood by a parody. Some devout Christian, let us say, has been set the task of translating the first sentence of *The Communist Manifesto* of Marx and Engels in such a manner that it will not disturb the calm of the faithful. It comes out, 'And God said, Unite ye poor and lowly and be not afraid for thou shall lose nothing but thy fetters, which by the grace of the Lord shall be struck from thy limbs.'

The sages had made use of the word 'Brahman' and that came in very useful. It could be made to sound like the Brahminical god. Words slipped in here and there could strike a religious note which would drown out the agnosticism which echoes throughout the text. Even, it would appear, whole verses could be manufactured. All this was done, but the Upanishads proved too strong for such obfuscations. When the Sanskrit scholars had finished, the teaching still shone through.

Centuries later the contrast shone even more clearly, and the best brain of the time felt that something should be done about it. The best brain of all was that of a philosopher, Sankara. He pointed out, in works of great intellectual brilliance, how the conflict could be resolved. He set up a school of philosophy known as the Vedanta, or the summit of the Vedas. It is the Vedanta which is taught in ashrams today, so we shall hear more of it in the course of this book.

But let us here get as close to the original as we can. There is one Upanishad which escaped almost unaltered, possibly because it is of very great beauty. It is the Katho Upanishad, but known popularly as the Upanishad of Nacheketas, its appealing central character.

Nacheketas is a boy of nine, a Brahmin and the son of a Brahmin. His father is an old man and is preparing for the fourth and final stage in his ordered life which, as we have seen, consists in giving away his worldly goods and retiring to a hermitage. It might be surmised that a goodly number of old men would try to dodge the rigours of this rule, as naturally as we try to dodge death-duties. The sages who taught this Upanishad thought so too.

In a few brief lines which are dazzling in their literary power, we are given portraits of the old man and the boy. Nacheketas's father is giving away his cattle to the Brahmins, who have gathered in great numbers to receive their gifts.

Nacheketas has all the simple, unquestioning faith in the religion he has been brought up in. He also has the discerning eye of a small boy.

His father is giving away his cattle and little Nacheketas observes, ironically, in the words of the text: 'These cattle have drunk water for the last time, eaten grass for the last time, yielded all their milk and are barren.' He wonders what sort of heaven his father will go to when he dies, since he is plainly cheating the Brahmins.

Now the rule prescribes that an elderly man going into retirement from the world should give *all* he has. So Nacheketas goes to his father and says:

'Father, to whom are you giving *me*?'

It is a barbed question. A father is not required to give his son away, but Nacheketas has neatly drawn attention to his father's meanness in bequeathing cattle which are tottering on their last legs.

His father is embarrassed by his son, as only small boys in public can embarrass their parents. He does not answer, but his temper is rising. Nacheketas asks him the question again; again he gets no answer. He asks it yet again. His exasperated father turns on him and roars at him, 'Drop dead!' Or, as the Sanskrit has it: 'I give you to Death.'

Instantly the small boy finds himself outside the portals of the Kingdom of the Dead. So far the poem has been kept on a high level of satire and swift action. Now come three stanzas so flatfooted in their propaganda as to be comic. According to one of the greatest of Sanskrit scholars, Max Müller, they are a later insertion. It is obvious that, in the original, Nacheketas finds himself suddenly in the presence of the God of Death, a terrifying confrontation, for in Hindu mythology the God of Death was a towering giant with a noose in his hand for capturing the souls of the dying and taking them off to their fate.

In the interpolation, Nacheketas is kept waiting outside the doors of the Kingdom of the Dead for three days. When they are finally opened by Yama, the God of the Dead, the God apologizes, and takes the occasion to preach a little sermon on the virtues of being hospitable to Brahmins. He orders water to be brought to the boy and admonishes the world at large: he enumerates the good luck a Brahmin can bring to a house – good company, good talk, successful sacrifices, sons and cattle – and observes that an ignoramus who does not feed his Brahmin guest will get none of them. The interpolation gets positively ludicrous as the huge Yama says to the little boy, 'Oh Brahmin, you a venerable guest have dwelt in my house for three days without eating.' (He has, in fact, been outside it.) 'Therefore choose three boons.' Yama then prostrates himself.

Nacheketas keeps his head admirably in front of this spectacle and, fortunately for us, we return to the original text.

The boy assumes that Yama will send him back to the living. His first request is movingly human. Fathers are fathers, sons are sons: he asks that when he gets back his father will welcome him, and not be angry any more. Yama agrees. He promises that the boy's father will sleep peacefully at nights and not be angry with Nacheketas for running away.

For his second boon Nacheketas asks, how, when he really dies, can he get to heaven? Here the interpolator gets busy with his stylus again. Obviously, it can only be done with a ceremony, so Yama describes, in detail, how he must build an altar, light a fire and sacrifice three times. There is some mumbo-jumbo about the significance of the number three. Then, like a stream running clear after being muddied, we are back again to the original.

Nacheketas, with great simplicity, makes his last request:

'There is this doubt about a man being dead. Some say he *is*: some say he is not.' He asks Yama to explain.

Yama echoes the sceptics. 'Even the gods of olden times have had their doubts about this,' he says. 'Ask me another boon. Do not press me to answer. For my sake, give up the question.'

But Nacheketas will not give up. If the old gods doubted, then there is nobody who can answer his questions but the God of Death himself. *He* must know, and what boon could be greater than his answer?

Yama names some.

'Choose sons and grandsons who will live to a hundred years,' he says to the boy. 'Choose herds of cattle, elephants, horses and gold. Choose any place on earth to live, and choose how long you may wish to live there. Live there as a king surrounded by fair maidens in their chariots, and music.'

Nacheketas's answer rises to the heights of poetry.

'Why', he says, 'even the longest life must end sometime. Then the chariots, the dance, the music, will all be yours. Settle my doubts. Tell me what lies beyond. I ask no other boon than to know that which is hidden from me.'

Yama yields. To put aside the pleasures of the world in order to gain knowledge is, he says, the first step towards gaining that knowledge, and Nacheketas has taken it. He begins to teach the boy about the true self.

In doing that, he strikes out a phrase that has become famous. 'If the slayer thinks "I slay" and if the slain thinks "I am slain", then both of them do not know well. This slays not nor is this slain.'

The thought is so attractive that it was quoted in later Hindu writings, including the Gita, from where it passed to the West. It has an air of mystery about it, as though there is some common bond between the killer and his victim. But the meaning is quite simple. The real self of the killer is unaffected by his act: the real self of the killed is untouched by his fate.

Why? The explanation is quickly forthcoming. This real self, says Yama, is to be found in the heart of each living being, in a cavern as it were, or a space within the heart. To know it Nacheketas, and any other seeker, must free himself from using his mind. He must give up willing and wishing. Yama goes on to the main point of the new teaching.

'This real self', he says categorically, 'cannot be attained by the study of the Vedas.' So much for the Brahmins. 'Nor', he goes on, 'can it be attained by intelligence.' So much for the philosophers, or any intellectual of whatever caste or race. 'And it cannot be attained by hearing.' So much for the sages of the Upanishads and their 'sit close beside me'.

It is, of course, not Yama who is speaking. He is merely a literary fiction. It is the sage himself who is speaking, dismissing himself as he does so. It is a key incident. To grasp its meaning, one should imagine a professor of today, famous for his learning in some special subject, saying to a pupil, 'By all means come to my lectures. But remember, I can teach you nothing. I admit that if I cannot teach you, nobody else can. All the same, you will not get what you want by listening to me.' Such a professor does not exist, except, perhaps, in some Theatre of the Absurd.

Then how is Nacheketas to learn? 'By choosing to learn', says the sage Yama. 'By choosing to discover the real self.' It is a hard saying, but true. The psychoanalyst's patient chooses to sit on the couch. Until he does so, there is no point in his spending the money, and an honest psychoanalyst will tell him so. The desire to find that space within the heart must be there and it must be strong. There must be something of the urgency which Yeats captures in his famous line: '*I will arise and go now, and go to Innisfree.*'

Once Nacheketas has chosen (and he has done so by showing little interest in the riches of the world that Yama was ready to give him), he must conduct himself in a certain manner. Yama illustrates this by a metaphor. He must imagine a chariot. The chariot is his body. The horses are his desires, his lusts, his anxieties, his pleasures. The reins are *his mind*. The charioteer is his superior mind, his super-ego, if you will. This must tell his mind to curb his desires, and his super-ego must control his mind. Yama lists the things again – desires, mind, and intellect.

'And beyond the intellect', he says, 'is the Great Self.' Finally, Yama throws aside all metaphors and gets to the nub of the matter: 'When the senses are at rest, when the mind is at rest, when the intellect ceases functioning, that is the highest state.' Nacheketas will have found his true self. And that true self does not die.

All the principal Upanishads say the same thing. Some have been so altered by the Sanskrit scribes that their teaching is obscured. Some have clearly been recollected by reporters with muddled minds, and leave the reader as confused as the reporter. But everyone who studies them has one which seems to him to express the teaching most clearly. For many it is the Katho Upanishad, with its enquiring boy. For me this is not so. It lacks – at least as we have it now – a vital piece. We do not know what happened to Nacheketas. We have seen that he assumes he will go back to the world and a father who he hopes will be better tempered. But did he? Did Yama let him go? And if he did, how did he feel and act when he was once more in the world? Other Upanishads answer that question, particularly the Chandogya Upanishad. The answer is extraordinary.

The seeker has found, let us assume, that cavern in the heart, that space where his true self resides. That true self cares nothing for the world: it has stopped wishing, desiring, and even thinking. It has analysed the past life of the old self, and discarded it all. It is completely detached: it is utterly calm. It is not a person, and it has not a personal name. It is as though in a deep sleep and yet is fully aware. All this we know. What happens next?

Nacheketas gave up women and chariots. The Chandogya says explicitly that the seeker who has found his true self can go back into the world and enjoy both, together with anything else that takes his fancy. Having controlled his desires, there is no need for him to stay in a hermitage to keep them controlled. Obviously, the world will seem a shadow of itself as it was before he learned the truth. A man who has dismissed the pleasures of sex as irrelevant is not likely to make an ardent lover. But the seeker who has found, never loses the prize. He can return to that cavern in his heart, he can be his true self, whenever he wishes.

The dangers of this doctrine to those who believe in law, order, morality and taking serious things seriously, are plain.

Sankara

The Brahmins were aware of this, but they had bigger troubles on their hands. Gautama Buddha had also taught that a man should abandon his worldly desires and aim at a tranquil state, called Nirvana. But he had been born a prince and was honoured by other princes when he came back into the world from under the bo-tree. Perhaps this made him reluctant to upset the apple-cart. He enjoined a code of conduct on his followers which would have made them admirable citizens. A man or woman who never told lies and never used violence would be any tyrant's dream subject. They would not, it is true, have much use for the religion of the Brahmins, but that, at first, was not much of a disturbance. Buddha gathered his followers into monasteries, where they lived out their lives and troubled no one.

The monastic life has great attraction for the young, who are afraid of the world, and the old, who are tired of it. But of those who wish to join a monastery, very few can. There are wives and families to provide for. There is the fear of monotony. So they do not join, but admire those who have done so. In Italy, which is full of monasteries and convents, there is provision for such people. You can become, for instance, a tertiary Franciscan. On certain days you put aside your fine worldly clothes, and wear the coarse habit of the Little Brothers. You do good works, give to the poor, and at the end of your life you have the right to be buried dressed as a monk. It is supposed that, after seeing this, St Peter will beckon you out of the queue at the gates of Heaven.

After the Buddha's death, his monks became very popular. People were anxious to be temporary monks, wear the robe a while, and go back to daily life in a religious and charitable state of mind. Monasteries became fashionable: rulers of kingdoms were proud to stay in them from time to time. Buddhism was not, in its original form, a religion. It had no gods, and only the simplest of ritual. It was merely a way of life, or more precisely, a way of escaping from it.

Lion capital of Asoka column at Sarnath. (Archaeological Museum, Sarnath; photo Martin Hürlimann) >

But it looked like a religion and soon its followers turned it into one. It does not seem that it took long. St Francis, who preached complete poverty, found himself (to his dismay) a rich man before he died. The newly-made Buddhist religion flourished likewise among the people.

It converted a king. He was Asoka, an energetic man who had already conquered a vast empire that took in most of the Indian peninsula. Having seen the light, he gave up killing animals for his table and killing people for the increase of his empire. He condemned wars of conquest, one of the very rare rulers in history to do so. A cynic might observe that there was precious little of India left to conquer, but there is no reason to doubt the sincerity of his conversion. He left monuments in the form of iron pillars all over the land, on which he admonished his subjects to follow the principles laid down by Gautama Buddha, and he may himself have spent some time in a monastery.

Until now, the Brahmins had been the advisers of kings and therefore their masters. Asoka retained the Brahmins, but their powers were much reduced. Whatever Nirvana was, it was obvious that the Brahmins were not needed to attain it.

The two religions existed side by side in peace, as they had to, since Asoka insisted on peace. To the Buddhists the Brahmins were misguided, but after all, theirs was the religion that their Founder had followed before he left for the forest, and it should therefore be respected. To the Brahmins, the Buddhists were just plain heretics. Asoka died and was followed by weaker kings, some less addicted to vegetarianism and universal peace than their great predecessor.

The Brahmins bided their time. Then, under rulers sympathetic to orthodoxy, they struck. The heretics were massacred inside and outside their monasteries, and the religion of the Vedas was restored.

All this took place at a time when Europe was in what is known as the Dark Ages. It is sobering to note that the Brahminical hegemony, once established, lasted down to the beginning of the twentieth century. It was a hegemony over the minds and souls of the Hindus, not over the actual land. That was twice conquered, in the major part: once by the Moslems, who despised all Hindus as idolators, and by the British, who despised the Hindus because they were so egregiously un-British. In all this long period there were no insurrections against the system. True, there were upsets: low-caste Sudras seized whole kingdoms, and ruled them, but always with the help of the Brahmins as advisers. As the nineteenth century drew to a close, various intellectuals attempted to form a new and more liberal faith: but their influence never went very deep, and their talkative little rebellions are now forgotten. When India became a free democracy,

< The 23-foot column of rust-free iron, dating back to the Gupta period, which stands before the arch in the courtyard of the Quwwat-ul-Islam Mosque in Old Delhi. (Photo Martin Hürlimann)

things changed, but, even in the 1970s, I have talked to Brahmins who ask in mystified tones why there is so much hostility towards them. Well-educated Brahmins who have travelled widely have told me, in all seriousness, that it is due to the disruptive influence of the Americans, aided by the nefarious schemes of the Central Intelligence Agency.

To be fair, it must be said that Brahminical orthodoxy was a success. Life in the lowest strata may have been a miserable affair, but then, so was the lot of a medieval peasant in Europe, to say nothing of the horrid existence of the Negro slave in America, or the factory worker in the Industrial Revolution. Above the lowest, all the way to the top, life was easy and luxurious. Curiously, nearly everybody in the West has nowadays had a glimpse of it. Every schoolboy has at least dipped into the *Kama-Sutra*. Apart from the dirty bits, which form only a small part of the book, it is a manual for a young man about town. It tells him what to wear, how to furnish his house, how to order his day, and how to seduce other men's wives. It bears a marked resemblance to such successful magazines as *Playboy*. We do not have the illustrations, but there is evidence that, at the time it was written, there was an ample supply of them.

The well-heeled, the landowners and their sons, the rich merchants, led lives of leisure, comfort and enjoyment. The others accepted their fates, and believed the priests, who told them that it was all due to the sins they had committed in some previous incarnation. It may be difficult for us to understand how such a theory could be accepted by thinking men and women. But it is no more extreme than John Calvin's firm conviction – and he was a highly intelligent man – that God had predestined some people to eternal damnation.

In all this period, however, there remained the obstinate problem of the Upanishads. They were part of the Vedas. The Vedas were the holy word of the gods. They could not be wrong. Swamis and gurus, traversing America today in their planes and luxury cars, can still be heard teaching their disciples the very same thing.

Yet the Upanishads contradicted the Vedas, however much they had been interpolated and rewritten. There were several attempts to argue this away. Whole schools of philosophy were founded in order to do so. The ingenuity of the arguments is fascinating, but only to metaphysicians, and there are very few metaphysicians left among us today. But one among them was that man of outstanding abilities that I have previously mentioned. His name was Sankara, or, as some scholars prefer, Samkara or Samkaracharya. Hindu mysticism, indeed the modern Hindu mind, cannot be understood without taking into account what he wrote.

76

An Indian ascetic (Urdhrabahu) holding his hands in the air until they waste and die, revealing an astonishing power of self-mastery. (Gouache from Murshidabad, Bengal, c. 1780–90; photo India Office, London) >

Like Nacheketas, he had an enquiring disposition even at the tender age of nine. Also like the boy in the Upanishads, he had an unsympathetic parent, in this case his mother. He wanted to become a wandering devotee, with saffron robe and begging bowl, but his mother would not hear of it. A charming legend says that one day he and his mother were bathing together. Then a crocodile seized Sankara by the foot. The boy profited by the occasion to ask his mother once again to let him be a devotee: only when she agreed did the crocodile let him go. The crocodile was, of course, a god in disguise, sent to teach Mother a lesson. Little boys may well envy Sankara's influential manner of getting his own way.

Regrettably, most of the other facts about his life were equally doubtful. He lived, according to the latest researches, between AD 788 and 838. On the other hand he may have died at the age of 32, or, again, lived until he was a very old man. A vast outpouring of books occupied his whole life, however long or short it was. Some which bear his name he certainly wrote. Others he did not. Most famous among the genuine ones were his commentaries on the Upanishads and the Bhagavad Gita.

He was the perfect man to bridge the gap between the Vedas and the Upanishads. He was a Brahmin, and an enthusiastic one. The old gods of the Vedas had been long forgotten. Others had taken their place. The two principal ones were Vishnu, a benign deity, and Siva, a great and powerful god with a complicated mythology behind him, representing the male power of pro-creation and capable, when he wished, of destroying mankind. Sankara wrote hymns to these gods and to their consorts. He was particularly devoted to Siva.

Like all zealots, he was also a reformer. The worship of Siva had, in some sections of the community, become degraded. A sect called the Kapilikas had introduced a mode of worship which, though sincere, included acts of quite remarkable obscenity. The roots of all this lay deep in the past, perhaps even before the Aryans came to India, as I shall show in a later chapter when I deal with Tantrism. Sankara attacked these abuses with contumely, an act typical of his character.

There is a story told about him as a young man: parts of it are obviously inventions, but it throws light on an important side of his make-up. While he was still studying he held debates with a famous pandit called Mandana. Such debates were something of a sport in those times, and a keen interest was taken in them. Mandana's wife acted as the referee and was responsible for declaring the winner. It soon became clear that her husband was getting the worst of the argument. She thereupon propounded a series of questions about sex, feeling

< Vishnu, the Preserver or Penetrator, in a South Indian form as Vardarja. (Bronze, Chola period, Central Museum, Madras)

sure the innocent student would know nothing about it. Sankara was not so easily beaten. Summoning up the help of his friends the gods, he transferred himself into the body of a voluptuous monarch, acquiring at the same time the king's wives and concubines, together with his expertise in keeping them happy. For three weeks he made love in various fashions. It does not appear that he was greatly attached to his new toys, for hearing some of his friends sing a holy song, he abandoned them, returned to the debate, and answered all the questions in such a decided manner that Mandana and his wife both became his awe-struck disciples.

Sankara was a puritan. All his life he detested the body and all its works, and this told heavily when he came to his commentaries on the Upanishads.

The problem was plain. The Upanishads said that the ultimate thing was the real self, which embraced the whole universe. This left no room for a worshipper and his God. This Self had been called two names, the Atman and Brahman. An easy solution was to confuse Brahman with the Supreme God, and thus satisfy orthodoxy. This had been done by some schools of philosophy, but it is greatly to Sankara's credit that he would have nothing to do with this sleight-of-hand. In a series of analyses, which are a delight to read for their clarity and penetration, he showed beyond any doubt that if there was a god, then the Upanishads said that it was the Atman, in other words, oneself. 'You', he said 'are Vishnu and Siva, provided you find out who you really are.' It is an idea which is very difficult to hold in the mind, and perhaps it can only be grasped when the mind has been still in the way that Yama told Nacheketas. Modern swamis and gurus, while doing reverence to Sankara, frequently dodge this central part of his teaching in many ingenious ways.

Sankara added a touch of his own character. He inveighs, with puritan zeal, against all bodily pleasures. The original sages were by no means so fervent. The urges of the body had to be controlled, it is true, while the search for the real self was going on. But, as we have seen, when the researcher has reached his goal, he can return to the world and enjoy it.

The thought of this disgusted Sankara, and in his summing-up of his beliefs he makes it quite clear that the searcher who still feels any lust for bodily pleasures has failed in his mission. Swamis and gurus, cut off from such delights by their profession, often make much of this, more than the Upanishads warrant. The great name of Sankara is often quoted in their aid.

Statues of Shiva and his consort, Parvati, from Elephanta (see pages 15 and 59). >

The Bhagavad Gita

Will it work? At this point of our enquiry, we have a fair idea of what the sages of the Upanishads taught. It is not very complicated – the sages repeated themselves over and over again, but we need not do the same. We also know the organized society against which they rebelled, and its parallel with our own is obvious. The notion of discovering the real self is attractive; the peace of mind, or, better, the peace of mindlessness is alluring in a tormenting world.

But few people are ready to leave the world, bad as it is. The Upanishads say you can leave it for a while, and then come back to it. What would be the result of this transcendental holiday? From earthly vacations one comes back bronzed. That soon fades. Will that happen in this case? If not, how shall I behave, how shall I look? Shall I have a halo, or – no, what is the word? – an aura?

I must admit that a generation or two ago there were many mystics who would have jumped at that last question, assuring the enquirer that he certainly would have an aura, and draw attention modestly to their own. Few Indians were of this stamp, but many of their Western followers were. The fashion for auras and that drawing-room version of mysticism has gone out with the ouija-board. Those people were fond of quoting bits of a book called the Bhagavad Gita. We must look into it, for the Gita has come back into fashion with such a bang that you can find people literally dancing in the streets about it, not only in Indian cities, but in London and New York.

The words Bhagavad Gita mean 'the song of the Lord', the Lord being the Hindu deity, Krishna. Its literary origins are mysterious. It is found at the climax of the long epic, the Mahabharatha, which otherwise is full of intriguing kings, mighty warriors, deep-plunging gamblers and the like. The epic is full of action and exciting to read, especially when some long digressions are skipped. The Gita is not a digression, but it is out of tone with the hearty action of the story. It is rather as though the warriors of the Iliad, just when they were girding for the

Krishna and the Gopi (cowgirl). (Indian miniature, mid-seventeenth century, India Office Library, London ; photo Fleming) >

final battle for Troy, had sat down with some early Socrates for a long, quiet philosophical talk.

The Gita is a poem, and one of great beauty. The reader is swept along in a stream of words, now running gently, now turbulent, now dashing with a mighty roar among the rocks. It has been translated into many languages and its beauty survives: even a poetaster rises above himself when he translates the Gita. There are a dozen versions in English. As a poem, then, the Gita is beyond praise: as a historical document it is a puzzle.

It was clearly written after the Upanishads for it leans heavily upon the ideas of the sages. Logically it must have been written before Sankara, because he wrote a commentary on it. But the Gita is so much in accord with Sankara's ideas, that the theory has been put forward that he himself wrote it, or, at least, altered it. Another theory, less drastic, is that it is a compilation by two or more hands. Certainly there are parts of it that are so contradictory that only the magnificent sweep of the language holds it together: but, for two or three readings, it does that very well. In analysing it, I shall hurt the feelings of some of its ardent admirers, many of whom it reduces to tears. But for our purpose here, it must be done.

The setting is a battlefield. The two opposing armies are waiting for the battle to begin. Their quarrel is a dynastic one. Friend is opposed to friend, relative to relative. Should the battle begin, it is inevitable that the principals will kill someone they love, or someone they have revered from childhood. The thought troubles Arjuna, a stalwart young hero who is certain to wreak wide slaughter should he do battle, for he is acknowledged as being the deadliest bowman alive.

He is in a chariot, and his driver is the god Krishna. That the gods were accustomed to take lowly disguises we have seen from Sankara's crocodile. Krishna is armed with a discus which, when thrown, infallibly cuts off people's heads at the neck. This does not appear in the Gita – only later, when the battle has begun.

Krishna was, and remains, the most popular god in the Hindu pantheon. He was a charming and gay little boy (it is told) and, unlike Nacheketas, quite untroubled by questions of philosophy. His major problem was an inordinate fondness of eating curds. A favourite theme in Hindu art is that of the chubby little boy (coloured, according to the canon, blue) tied to a tree so that he cannot reach a bowl of his preferred food. Magically, the rope lengthens, and he gets what he wants.

He is a pastoral god, and a very realistic one. When he grows to be an adolescent, he falls in love with the girls who keep the cows. He enjoys their favours, and they his. Legend awards him six thousand lovers. As a young man, he performs

The Loves of Krishna. (Detail of a gouache painting on paper, Rajasthan, nineteenth-century. Collection Ajit Mookerjee, New Delhi; photo Jeff Teasdale) >

a number of titanic feats which so resemble the twelve labours of Hercules that it was once thought he is a product of Greek influence. It is now believed that it might have been the other way about, so much that is Greek having been found to have its origin in the East.

This, then, is Arjuna's charioteer – an immortal, and Arjuna knows it. With something of a flourish, Arjuna orders him to drive the chariot between the two armies, that he might examine them. Suddenly his courage fails him. Plunged into despair, he opens his heart to Krishna.

He does not want to kill his kinsmen. He does not want to bring ruin and despair to their families. The battle will be for a kingdom, but who would want a kingdom at such a price. 'I would rather', he says, casting down his bow, 'eat the food of a beggar than eat royal banquets tasting of their blood.'

The problem is one of our own times. Krishna the god answers it precisely in the terms of a middle-aged hawk admonishing a young dove who is threatening to tear up his draft card. After a quick run-through of some elevated thoughts from the Upanishads, he gets down to business. Of course, Arjuna must fight. He would be dishonoured if he did not, and dishonour is worse than death. Arjuna is not convinced, which is reasonable because Krishna, quoting the Upanishads, has said that for the spirit there is no death, especially if a man has taken thought and found his real self. Arjuna, with soldierly bluntness, points out the contradictions. What, he asks, is this business of taking thought and finding immortality?

Krishna begins in a thoroughly orthodox manner. The Vedas ask for sacrifices: sacrifices imply action, for action is prescribed by the Vedas as the proper destiny of man. Arjuna is a good Brahmin. Arjuna must fight. He must do his own duty. 'To die in one's duty is life: to live in another's is death,' Krishna says in a somewhat sententious epigram.

Arjuna has pricked up his ears. Krishna has mentioned men who find salvation by action, works according to the Vedas, and sacrifices. But he has also mentioned another sort of Yogi who reaches the same end by renunciation, a Upanishadic teaching. Arjuna wants to know which is the better, a good question, because the man who has renounced the possibility of works cannot do them.

Krishna answers squarely that the finer of the two is renunciation. But renunciation means a man who has attained inner tranquillity. We can see where he is heading (we have been there before in the preceding pages) but it is surprising to see him suddenly take the plunge. 'Such men', he says, 'can look with equal affection on a Brahmin, a cow, an elephant, or a dog, even a man who eats a dog.'

Now eaters of dogs (and much, much worse) were members of a sect of heretics who did it to spite the Brahmins. It is a pregnant statement, especially from one who, a few verses before, had recommended obedience to the Vedas. Krishna goes on to tell of the man who finds his true self, and of his peace.

But if, says Krishna, a man does not choose this path, then he must work in the world as though he wanted to. He must work without any desire for gain, or reward, or praise, because he knows that these are all inferior things. He must control his mind when he leans towards them, because only by this discipline can he arrive at the higher thing, the discovery of himself. We are, then, in the realm of the Upanishads in all their purity.

Now the narrative takes a turn. 'Who is the self, this Brahman?' Krishna asks. 'I am he,' he answers, 'I, the Lord Krishna.' We are still near the sages: they taught that the true self embraced everything. The poetry now scales new heights. Krishna sings of all the beauties of the universe – the sun, the moon, the soul of man. He, the Lord, is the Father of everything.

The narrative takes a last turn, and the sages of the Upanishads fade into the distance – Krishna, having proclaimed his omnipotence, demands that all men love him. Peace is to be found in a passionate devotion to the Lord of Creation.

Krishna undergoes a transfiguration in front of Arjuna. He grows to an immense height. He is seen with all the attributes of Hindu godhead, including teeth in the grip of which writhe Arjuna's enemies.

Arjuna abases himself and worships the god of gods. He goes into battle because Krishna has told him to, and for no other reason.

Tantrism

The Gita ends on a note very familiar to the West, which may account for its popularity there – Arjuna worships the Creator, just as every Christian does when he goes to church. The poem begins with sound everyday common sense, goes on to the Upanishadic doctrines of the supremacy of the real self, and ends with chords on the organ and hymn-singing to God. It is correct that it does so. Simple, heartful worship of an unimaginably powerful deity seems to be a basic need of the vast majority of mankind in any age of history. The Upanishadic sages did not feel that need. Nor do a minority of people today.

But there is a difficulty for that minority. If the real self is everything, as the sages say, then any worship (if worship is needed) must be given to that very same self, an act which is somewhat odd. It can be done. My father did it all his life. A Hindu by birth, when he came to maturity he had no use for any organized religion. But he had read the Upanishads, and almost his last request to me before he died* was that I should do the same.

On the wall of his bedroom, for as long as I remember, was an enlarged photograph of himself, dressed in Edwardian style, surrounded by a wide, ornate frame. He had written out a number of prayers, which were in a small leather-bound book. Every morning he would take this little breviary between his hands, and pray for some five minutes to his own picture. He was not, let me add, vain: he was modest to a fault. He was merely doing what, from an Upanishadic point of view, was philosophically, theologically and morally the right thing to do.

Yet it was a pretty bleak thing to watch. I preferred the morning service when I got to my Anglican school, when I could thank a highly personal God in a thumping good hymn-tune, and pray to His attentive ear that the Latin master would not find out that I had skimped my homework.

*See my autobiographical essay *The Space Within the Heart*, London and New York 1971.

88

This need for a personal deity was naturally felt by Indians. Siva, Vishnu and Krishna met it to some extent. But the Brahmin priests, like children in a large family, were always there. Fees had to be paid them, so that worship became a part – and no small part – of the household budget. Buddhism brought in a warmer note, but that was swept away. It seemed that the Brahmins now had everything their own way; but there was a warm, even hot, faith waiting in the wings.

This was Tantrism. When the English discovered the existence of this religion in India they were horrified. To this day they have left the impression that it is a sort of obscene voodoo. One of the hymns I used to sing at school spoke of Ceylon's coral isle, 'where every prospect pleases/And only man is vile.' Vile meant Tantrism. I got considerable credit among my schoolfellows by pretending that I had knowledge of its secret and disgusting practices, until they found out that I did not.

My ignorance was excusable. Very few people do know anything about it. A great number of its texts have been destroyed by the orthodox Hindus: those that remain are so complicated that I would have given up reading them, had they not had a bearing on the subject of this book. Tantrism affected Hindu mysticism, especially in the matter of Yoga.

There is much dispute about its origins. It is not found in the broad landmass of India today. It survives only in the far north-east, amid the jungles and foothills of the Himalayas. Since we know that the pre-Aryan Indians were driven to this area, some think it may be a survival of the original faith of the country. I doubt this: there is no proof. Some of its black magic may have its roots among primitive people; the rest not only suggests a sophisticated civilization, there is even a smell of decay of that civilization about it. Whatever its remote origins may be, we pick it up, historically, about the time of the rise and fall of the Buddhists. We can be sure of this, because the later Buddhists adopted some of the Tantric symbols.

Among the orthodox Hindus, the worship of the great gods Siva, Vishnu and (perhaps) Krishna held sway. These gods had wives, and in particular Siva. The Tantras, like the Vedas, are collections of verses. Like the Vedas, they have elaborate directions for the right way to worship. But in their case, the object of devotion is not the male god, but his wife. The followers of Tantra were admirers, to the point of frenzy, of Woman, in all her aspects, the cruder the better. The apotheosis of Woman was the Mother, and the Tantric abased himself before Motherhood in a way that was not to find a parallel until twentieth-century America. The Tantric devotee longs for Mother to take him on Her lap. He

The gods were thought to have both male and female attributes, as in this representation of Shiva, from Elephanta. >

yearns for the security of being between Her breasts, except when he is begging to suck Her milk.

He believes in meditation, but I would not call it very transcendental. The devotee should concentrate on some object which is of importance to him. A woman's sexual organs are a highly suitable point of concentration, especially when combined with the mental picture of their being penetrated by the penis. Sex generally is of the highest importance. All human beings are composed by two principles, the male and the female, a notion which should not be confused with the Chinese Yin and Yang, though it may well have given rise to it. The gods are similarly made up of two parts, male and female. Statues exist, showing this, the right side of the god being masculine, the left having an ample female buttock, and a breast.

It follows as the night the day that the best way of being godlike is to have intense sex with a woman. Nirvana can be attained by having sex to the point of utter exhaustion. So far, the Tantric teaching is comparatively simple, but complications follow.

One Tantric sect believed that the male devotee, to complete himself, must think of himself as a woman. He should walk like her, speak like her, have her emotions, and dress like her. Then again, some men, by nature, are more feminine than male, and these are particularly holy. They are of several sorts: there is the eunuch, *tout court*, there is the hermaphrodite, there is the neuter whose sex has dried up, and so on. The normal devotee, in his search for sexual experience, can have it with these, and derive spiritual benefit.★

Since the sexual act, in its multifarious forms, was also religious, it had to be done in the best ways possible. Nor was there any particular reason why it should always be done in private. Tantrism studied the various postures of sex, and devotees performed it in certain major temples. Victorian missionaries, horrified to find that the abominations of the Canaanites were not confined to the pages of the Bible, fumed that this faith should be extirpated forthwith. Neither the people, nor, to its credit, the British government, lifted a finger to help them. It is ironic that in the lands from which these missionaries came, children are now taught in school that there is fulfilment in well-managed sex, their parents make love in the presence of others, sometimes with diverse other parents, and homosexuality is considered harmless between those who like it. One description of fulfilment to be found in the texts is particularly amusing. To gain the maximum benefit, the principal devotee is advised to let a woman fellate him, while a pupil desirous of sharing the experience can do so by pushing a finger up the

★Very little Tantrism has survived in contemporary India, but it would seem that the eunuchs have done so. One of India's most distinguished poets, Kamala Das, has described an experience of them, on which she based a poem:

'The poem – Eunuchs – got written in the summer of 1963 when I had returned to Calcutta after staying away for twelve years. One day at about 11 in the morning I called on my mother's friend whose daughter-in-law had given birth to a baby son a week ago. They lived in Raja Basanta Roy Road in an old pink scarred building. The eunuchs came to the gate and said that they wanted to dance to celebrate the arrival of the baby. The master of the house said, "No, I don't want anyone to dance for this baby." Then he shut all the windows of the drawing-room. For about half-an-hour the eunuchs kept banging on the door and shouting abuses in their harsh voices. My host put some records on to drown their voices. The eunuchs cursed the baby. They cursed every member of the family. "I don't believe in these customs," the host said. "I think these old customs are meaningless." His wife agreed with him.

'I bade farewell and left the house by a backdoor, hoping to see the eunuchs' group. They were dancing in front of another house. I parked the car near the kerb and watched them. The dancers wore red lipstick and rouge. They made coquettish gestures. The more masculine-looking ones sat in a row behind the dancers, thumping on their little drums.'
(quoted p. 14, Subhas C. Saha, *Insights*, Calcutta 1972).

worshipper's anus. This adolescent fantasy can nowadays be found described in pornographic books in a thousand shops in the West.

I hope therefore to be understood when I say that, so far, Tantrism is innocent. It would have no importance in the study of mysticism if it were not for two contradictory developments. The first of these maintained that wild abandonment to sex led the worshipper to gain magical powers. The other school agreed that semen was of the greatest importance, but to gain magical powers it should be retained. We may call these the permissive school and the restrictive school.

I have hitherto avoided making the pages of this essay into a leopard-skin of Sanskrit words spotting English prose. English is a rich and varied language and most Hindu concepts can be expressed in it without an army of parentheses. But now we come upon some notions which cannot: they are too remote from the Anglo-Saxon experience.

There is the concept of Siddhi. This says that a man who devotes himself to the pursuit of knowledge attains a special power, provided he performs certain acts. These range widely. He may take drugs, he may inflict austerities upon himself, he may do certain acts which outrage ordinary morality. He may, above all, perform Yoga. The person doing these things is called a Sadhaka, and if he succeeds in his aim becomes a Sadhu. The Tantric texts are addressed to Sadhakas.

The Siddhis are attainments, or powers, of an uncommon nature. Once attained, the devotee can use them to make himself as big as the universe, or as small as an atom. He can make himself as heavy as a mountain, or so light that he can fly to the moon. He can create, or destroy, both inert matter and living creatures. He has some minor, but useful, abilities. He can turn metals into gold, fly through the air with or without his body and, most conveniently, he can be in two places at once, or even more than two places. Some such thing is necessary to the full satisfaction of his desires, because he is irresistible to women, and his prowess with his penis is stupendous.

Another way of acquiring Siddhi is by means of the Kundalini. It is a serpent that sleeps in three coils: we are warned that, in tampering with it, we are on dangerous ground.

According to the Tantric texts, we all have it. It sleeps in that area of our bodies which is called the crotch, extending to the rectum. If we wish to awaken it, we can do so by assiduously practising certain forms of Yoga. It awakens little by little. It uncoils and we feel it advancing up our spine like hot water. At each stage it releases vast powers within us. Our skin burns, we sweat, we feel as though an insect is stinging us. The Siddhis we acquire from the snake are so powerful they

can destroy us if we are not in full control of them. The Kundalini rises and rises. Just where its limit is, the seers dispute. But when it has reached that limit, we are suffused with bliss.

Let us now leave the snake sleeping safely in our bottoms, and turn to another way of gaining supernatural powers. This is antinomianism, or, in a rather more ear-catching phrase, Yoga through Bhoga, the last word meaning 'Do What Thou Wilt'. The Tantras are quite specific about it. A man, to gain salvation and Siddhis, must do anything that comes into his head, but particularly those things which are usually regarded as sinful.

To upset and outrage respectable society has always had great merit. But the Tantric rebellion is curiously adolescent in its style. It has a teen-age fascination with breaking the sexual code with women. Nothing conduces to the acquisition of magical powers more than going with prostitutes or seducing another man's wife. The use of obscene words is recommended. Living should be as simple as possible, away from the corruption of cities, and out into the fresh air of the countryside. The hippy movement in our own times has much in common with this outlook. In this form, Yoga through Bhoga can be dismissed as naughty but charming.

It is another matter when we come to the most famous antinomian of them all. His name was Gorakhnath: he lived in the eleventh century and was a member of the sect of Nathas. The etymology of his name is disputed, but the commonest derivation is The Lord of Filth. It is a description in which he gloried. Although his tenets were founded in religion, his aims were to gain magical powers to work both good and evil. All the world knows that Hindus treat the cow as sacred. Gorakhnath ate it, and told his followers to do the same. All the world knows that the Hindus are meticulous about their diet: Gorakhnath approved the eating of faeces. The eating of corpses was not disapproved of. Sexual union with animals was considered a useful step in gaining occult powers. As a result of these austerities, he and his followers were feared by all as magicians who knew how to wreak incalculable harm on whomever they wished, from inflicting him with diseases to killing him outright by necromancy.

The sadhu, I have said, is one who is an adept and attained supernatural powers. Something of the fear which surrounded Gorakhnath and his followers still surrounds the sadhu today, at least in the countryside. He is distinguished by his saffron robe and begging bowl, or, in some cases, by the bowl alone, for some go stark naked. For a barren woman to touch the sadhu's penis is held to be a guarantee of a child. He sells charms and amulets and magical medicines. He sometimes gathers together with other sadhus to form vast processions at religious festivals.

< *Yogini with serpentine energy; south India, c. 1800. Collection Ajit Mookerjee, New Delhi.*

Sadhus are wandering holy men, who may own nothing more than a robe, a staff, beads and a begging bowl.

They are believed to have magical powers, and sell magic potions and charms, and tell fortunes.

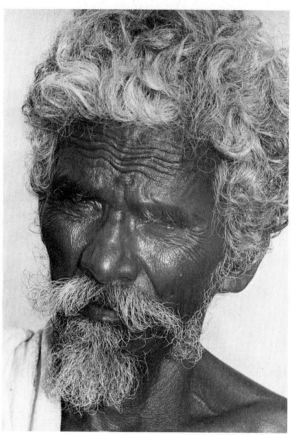

Three typical sadhus of contemporary India.

He is detested by the orthodox Hindu and persecuted by the police, who treat him as a beggar, a charlatan and a trouble-maker. Large gatherings are periodically banned and, if formed, broken up. The sadhu, regarded as a romantic figure in the Western world, is considered a pest in contemporary India.

Tantrism and all its works have fallen into disrepute. Foreigners, like myself, who retell its history are much disapproved of. In practice there is little of it left, except in remote parts. India is respectable: marriages are still arranged by the parents of both parties; lovers are disapproved of, except on the cinema screen, where a rigid censorship forbids them to be seen kissing, much less doing all the other things we are accustomed to seeing in the West.

But Tantrism cannot be ignored. It has left a legacy which, precisely in that unbridled Western world, has an innocent following. Gorakhnath wrote a treatise on Hatha Yoga, and it is to Yoga we must now turn our attention.

Above, and on pages 104–7, are examples of simple Yoga postures and exercises, which may be used as an introduction to meditation. They tone up the muscles and aid respiration, which should never be forced.

Yoga

Although it may disappoint romantics, the proper translation of the word Yoga is 'curriculum'. That is all it means. A curriculum is a series of studies which a person must go through if he wishes to attain a certain knowledge – a degree, for instance. The literal translation of the Sanskrit is 'a bridge', with the understanding that it is a bridge to learning about the true self.

There are several sorts of Yoga. The one that is, in fact, recommended by the sages is Raja Yoga. This resembles the curriculum of a place such as the Princeton Institute of Advanced Studies. It merely says you must spend a certain amount of time thinking, if you have the brains to do it. The God of Death took the boy Nacheketas through a rapid course of Raja Yoga. The description of the path towards realizing the true self, which will be found in the early chapters of this book, is pure Raja Yoga. It is not particularly difficult. Sumerian studies, or the decipherment of the Linear B script from Knossos are not impossibly difficult things, provided you have time and solitude.

But as any Indian will tell you (if put to it), time to think in solitude has always been, for immemorial ages, one of the rarest things in India. It is a country of large families. Moreover, it is a country of strange affairs called the joint family, in which, when the children grow up and marry, they live under the same family roof, husband going to his wife's family house, or vice-versa, according to which roof is the most commodious. Children are owned, loved, cared for or beaten by any member of the whole crowded nest. The present Prime Minister of India (1973) was brought up in a joint family, until the British Raj broke it up by putting sundry members of it in jail. Even today, doors in an Indian family are rarely locked.

This was even more true of the Indian family household in the days of the Vedas and the Upanishads. Indians look back on these times as a golden age (Ram Raj it is called) when a man was always in the bosom of his family. It is reasonable to suppose that at least some of the old men went off into the jungle as prescribed with a certain amount of thankfulness.

Old men *are* old: their mind is no longer nimble. They may want to meditate on the fundamental things, but they want even more to have the occasional refreshing nap. Little in the way of intellectual penetration can be expected of a man who has spent his life in the midst of his relatives every hour of the day.

The system that coped with this situation was Yoga. It was an exercise by which a man could be alone in the corner of a house swarming with people. Even the brashest youngster would hesitate about interrupting someone fixedly staring at the point of his own nose with both eyes (the classic Yoga pose, recommended by all its teachers). The sages of the Upanishads adopted a practice which was already in existence before they started their teaching.

Yoga may very well have been practised even before Vedic times: it may have been part of the pre-Aryan faith. It was not, in origin, a bridge to realize the true self. It was a system by which one could gain control of the body, thus obtaining those magical powers called Siddhis. The sages of the Upanishadic period showed no interest in this side of it. They took up Yoga and recommended it, but if they are read carefully it will be seen that their attitude towards it was no more mystical than that of schoolmasters: they advised a healthy mind in a healthy body. You would, in the end, abandon your mind and forget your body. But until that time, you would be advised to keep both in good working order.

Hence Hatha Yoga. Hatha Yoga enjoys a great vogue in the Western world, and the reason is easy to see. It satisfies the Western man's passion for physical exercise, while raising it above the level of the locker-room. The Indian is not enamoured of violent exercise: the climate discourages it. But like every other human being he is concerned about his health. The early postures of Hatha Yoga are more attractive than press-ups because they largely consist of just sitting in a position which, to the Indian, was comfortable, because he did not habitually use chairs.

It should be noted that Yoga in origin had nothing to do with religion. The Yogi did not try to meet the Creator. The first description we have of it is from Patanjali, who lived approximately at some time during the flourishing of the Roman Empire. In his book there is only an incidental mention of God, and that may be an interpolation.

Hatha Yoga then, is a physical exercise; like all exercise, it is beneficial when not carried to extremes. Rowing a boat is a similar exercise, and very pleasant. But a champion rower is a different matter. He performs marvels for his club, but it does not mean that he is a healthy man. If the marvels are very wonderful, he

B. K. S. Iyengar, one of India's best known teachers of the genuine Hatha Yoga. One of his pupils is Yehudi Menuhin.

may end up with a damaged heart. People who soberly practise Yoga rarely carry it to physical extremes. There is nothing to be gained from doing so. Teachers of Yoga are another matter. Like any other practised athlete they are not above showing off their prowess. The photographs of gurus in acrobatic poses are just that, and nothing more. Hatha Yoga for the general run is a gentle exercise much like golf, and a good deal less expensive, especially in clothing.

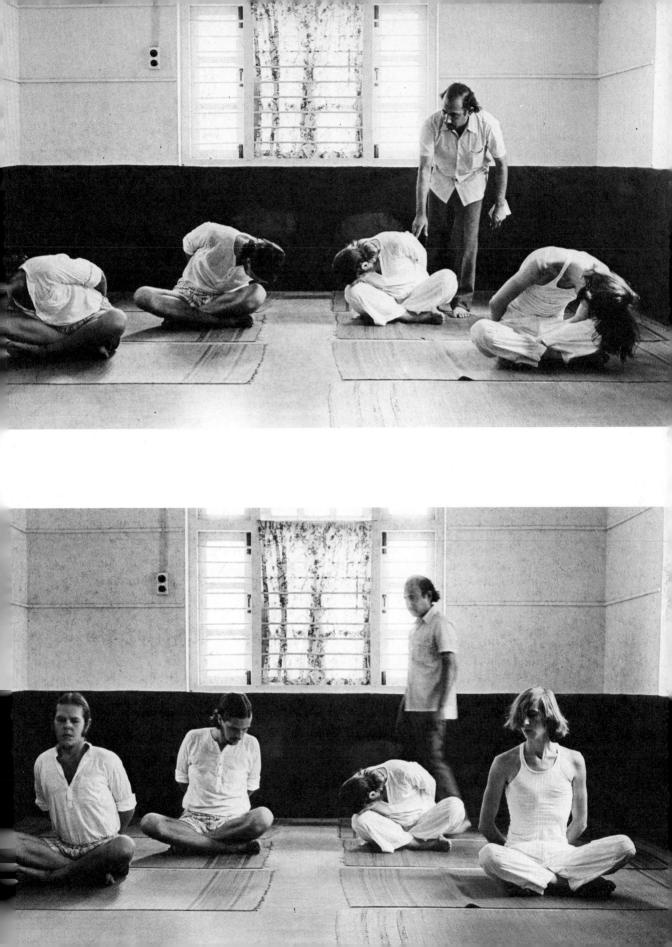

But the parallel must not be pressed too far. Golf is an exercise. So is Hatha Yoga. Golf is a sport and Yoga is emphatically not. Western sport had its origin in ancient Greece, where it was essentially a competition. Its practitioners strove to win. It was the winner who got the laurels and maybe a statue in the Agora, not the loser. There are people, I know, who strive to excel at Yoga. They are the despair of the honest gurus, and the joy of the charlatans.

In sport you worry about winning. In some team sports there are coaches who specialize in producing a state of worry which approaches hysteria. The aim of Hatha Yoga is the opposite. It trains your body and its internal organs so that they are in harmony. They function smoothly, so smoothly that you can forget them. A golfer, for instance, can never forget his body: if he does, he tops, slices or commits some other of that endless catalogue of faults to which a golfer is liable. If you try to stand on your head in Hatha Yoga and fall over, it does not matter. You will be required, when the exercise is over, to meditate quietly for a few minutes. You will not be required to meditate on how you can improve your headstands. The meditation should be as near to Raja Yoga as you can get. This is why the sages of the Upanishads, together with Gautama Buddha, turned their backs on austerities as a means to enlightenment. You cannot forget your body when your stomach is clamouring for a meal.

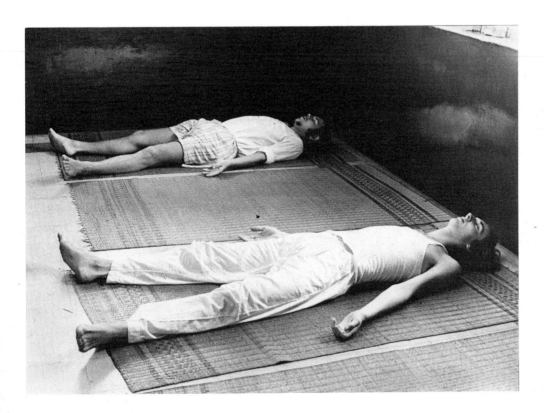

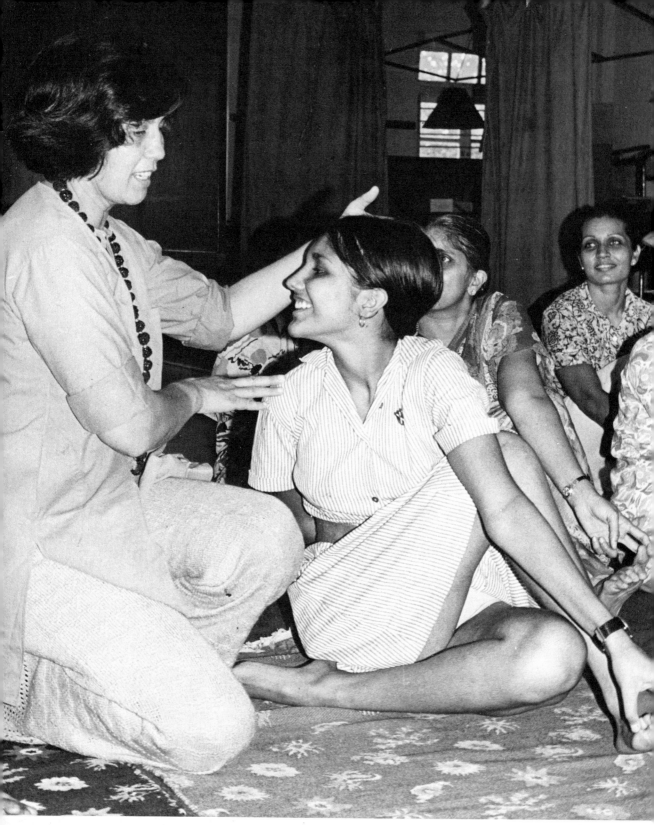

Swami Yogeshwarananda conducting a class in Hatha Yoga.

Swami Yogeshwarananda.

A side of Hatha Yoga which has attracted a lot of attention is breath-control. This forms part of the original teaching of Patanjali. It is easy to see why. All forms of Yoga aim at producing a state of tranquillity in the subject. It can, say the ancients, be done by drugs, but as we know today, drugs call for more drugs: the tranquillity does not last. The calming effect of breath-control can be attested by any wife observing her husband when he is engaged in a quarrel. His breathing is fast and irregular. The quarrel made up, he sleeps tranquilly by her side. He breathes more slowly. Or again, when he is lying under some tree or sun-umbrella on vacation, thinking of nothing in particular, his breathing is light.

In the same way, by slowing down the breath and diminishing its quantity, a calming of the nerves can be produced. Physiologically, of course, it is not the 'nerves' that are calmed (that is our manner of speaking). It is the mind. How, it is not clear. But so many people have now practised it, that it may be taken as being true.

I should stress once more that Hatha Yoga is not a sport. To attempt records at breath-control, to pit your will against your lungs, can be very dangerous. It can produce respiratory diseases which will permanently injure your health. Any good guru will tell his pupil so. It is one of the reasons (besides the money) that gurus say that Hatha Yoga should be practised under their guidance.

For a person of a strong-willed, competitive nature, this is undoubtedly so. For milder persons, who know enough to stop when they are tired or feeling dizzy, a guru is not necessary. Hatha Yoga itself is not necessary. Raja Yoga will do. But for centuries Hatha Yoga has been found to be fun: and to feel so well in your body that you can forget it is always desirable.

There are other Yogas. One of the most widely practised in India is that in which you still the mind by the constant repetition of a certain phrase or a verse from the scriptures. Mahatma Gandhi was a model of serenity in the middle of

Mahatma Gandhi : a statue at Santa Cruz.

the most violent political storms. He said more than once that it was this other discipline which supported him in trouble.

The repetitions chosen may be anything that pleases the person doing it. They vary in India from a single syllable (A U M or O M) to several words. As I have already mentioned, these are known as mantras, and I shall use the word because it is rapidly becoming as much part of the English language as guru, swami and so forth.

If much of Tantrism seems to be adolescent, the sight of devotees sitting in rows on the ground and repeating verses in unison is inclined, at first sight, to look infantile. On closer examination it is seen to be a Yoga which has been used for centuries in the West to induce mental concentration.

In Catholic churches there is a ceremony in which the congregation brings its rosaries and recites some simple mantras from the New Testament. In particular, the congregation, led by a priest, says over and over again the greeting which the Angel of the Annunciation gave to the Virgin: 'Hail Mary, full of Grace' and so forth. At each mantra the worshipper moves a bead of the rosary. Scattered round the rosary are bigger beads, and when these arrive a standard mantra in the form of a prayer is said. The rosary is usually recited in the early evening, and the congregation mainly consists of women who are busy mothers or wives. These are notoriously lacking in mental concentration, the variegated demands of family life making it impossible. But by this monotonous recital, they find it possible to relax their minds. Once relaxed, they can bring their thoughts to bear on religious things.

Or again: people who are not Catholics are often curious to know what exactly are the penances which a priest hands out to the faithful after they have confessed their sins. Nowadays, these are almost always an instruction to say mantras: the rosary must be gone through a certain number of times, while in church. The penitent is not asked to reflect on his or her sins. He is no longer a sinner; he has been absolved of these in the confessional. But the mantras must be said to still the mind.

Rosaries were in use in India long before they were introduced into the Catholic Church and there is some evidence that they may have been borrowed from there. Mantras are used in the regular Catholic liturgy. *Kyrie Eleison, Christe Eleison,* is a pure mantra; so is the long invocation of the name of the saints which forms part of the preparation of the faithful for Easter. The Pope, when he appears on holy days at his famous window, makes use of a mantra: he invites the crowd in the square below to recite the Angelus with him. It is a Yoga which, to judge the expressions of the people leaving the square, is very effective.

We now come to Bhakti Yoga, and a vexed question. It is well-known that the Catholic Church in its early years absorbed a number of beliefs that were current in the Roman Empire. Its primal ceremonies were very simple: a gathering of the faithful, some prayers, and a meal in commemoration of the Last Supper. This meal had none of the anxious solemnity of the later Mass. It was a meal to which one brought one's own vittles and ate them. It was a happy affair, so much so that St Jude felt called upon to warn the sisters and brothers not to make it too jolly.

But many of the converts had been used to the gorgeous ceremonies of the worship of Isis, or the heart-stopping ritual of the mystery religions. The Christian faith seemed a little bare. Christ was the Son of God: he called to the meek to worship, and the Church had to accommodate the demand. This was done by adopting much from other, more emotional religions.

The sages of the Upanishads did not set up a religion. They had no God. 'Brahman' was not the name of deity: it was the name of something you discovered in your self. There were statues of the orthodox god Brahma in abundance, some with three heads to show his various powers. But this Brahma was not (and it is often forgotten by gurus) the Brahman of the Upanishads. In fact, the sages had a good-humoured contempt for the gods of the populace. In one Upanishad they invent a story in which certain of the gods of the Vedas come to seek the ultimate wisdom from a sage, for all the world as though they were disciples of the rebels. The sage plays with them, fobbing them off with advice to dress themselves up in their finest clothes and look at themselves in a pool of water – there, he assures them, they will find the last truth. After one or two more japes of this sort, they grow suspicious. The sage, relenting, tells them of the space within the heart, the real self.

The gods are satisfied with this: but the people were not. Like early Christianity it seemed a bare faith. There was no room for worship. So the gods crept back. Philosophers like Sankara clung to the original austerity. Others did not. The ultimate reality was what the sages had said. The Upanishads were, after all, part of the Vedas; and the Vedas could not be wrong. Worship came back with the gods as a Yoga. Bhakti Yoga encouraged a passionate devotion to divine things – the gods and their wives. They were not the Supreme, the God of Gods; that was within the devotee. But worshipping them was a step along the path.

Bhakti Yoga thus became a part of the mysticism of the Upanishads, and still is for some sects, as we shall see. It is a contradiction, but contradictions have never troubled the Hindu. He makes his own *tutti-frutti* and is quite content with it. That is why Hinduism has endured for so long.

Hinduism at bay

So far, things had gone well for Hinduism. The beliefs that the Aryans had found in the land had been driven underground, to sprout up again here and there in the extravagances of Tantrism, but never as a widespread religion. Buddhism had come and gone, with only a few ruined mounds to show that it had ever existed. The rebels of the Upanishads had been absorbed into the Establishment. Their disturbing teachings had been buried under commentaries that purported to explain them, but, in fact, explained them away. Elaborate temples had been built for the worship of the great gods, Siva and Vishnu, while Krishna drew off the passion to adore among the broad masses of the people. Caste was so firmly established that any other way of life seemed mere libertinage. The Brahmin reigned supreme.

Then Hinduism was challenged by a religion which was not a *tutti-frutti* at all. In the deserts of Arabia, Mohammed, who could neither read nor write, had founded the religion of the Book. The Koran had been given him by an angel, inscribed on the shoulder-blades of sheep, and it was very precise. It had no room for idols or philosophers. There was one God, and he was not to be found by looking inside one's head. He was in Heaven, a place which Mohammed had visited by leaping from a rock in Jerusalem. His name was Allah, Mohammed was his prophet, and his commands were clear. He needed no elaborate Yogas, He called for daily prayers and utter obedience to His decrees. He knew the destiny of all who worshipped Him and they could not alter it by a jot or tittle. Their duty was to spread His faith throughout the world, sword in hand. Those of His warriors who fell in battle would go straight to Paradise. There they would find houris to attend to all their needs, spirits that were the only vague thing in the whole faith, because the warrior in repose could make them any shape or sex that took his fancy.

< *The great Shiva Temple, Chidambaram. (Photo Martin Hürlimann)*

His warriors went out with Book and Sword. They struck west and built an empire from Mecca to the Atlantic Ocean. They struck east and reached India, founding another empire. They smashed the idols of the Hindu gods and slew or converted their worshippers.

But India was a big place, and it was inhabited by a lot of people. Even today, with our weapons, it would be hard to kill all of them. The followers of the Prophet soon gave up trying to kill, or convert them. They compromised by taxing the Hindus up to their back-teeth with only some occasional idol-smashing to keep up the morale of the tax-collectors.

So far I have been unkind to the Brahmins. The world they made is not my world: I have always enjoyed freedom. But there, perhaps, lies my mental limitation. I have never lived under the heel of an alien conqueror. I have never faced men who ordered me to change my thoughts or be killed. That being so, I must give the Brahmin Establishment its due.

Its merit lay in just that word: it was established. The Moslems were not. As their empire widened, their morals went slack. From being the stern desert Arabs, spartan in their ways, they slowly dissolved into luxury and sloth. Their palaces, their jewelled swords, the legends of their harems and debauchery are still with us to tell of it. But the world of the Hindu did not change, because it could not. There was no provision for change. There were defectors from it: the Sword is a powerful argument for believing in the Book. But the converts went on living in the Brahmin framework. All Moslems are equal: the converts still observed the rules of caste. The humblest poor man, once embracing the Faith, can speak to the Caliph himself, as he often does in *The Arabian Nights*: the convert still shunned eating with the outcastes.

Those who stood firm and were not converted had another source of strength. In a great crisis, the narrow-minded man is often the winner. He cannot see that he can possibly be wrong, and may, in the end, turn out to be right. The Hindu could not conceive of a happy life outside the rules of the Establishment. His conquerors seemed to him to be misguided fools. Brought up to believe that one day he should give up all his luxuries, his women and his wealth, to go seeking the truth, he looked on the life of the Moghuls who ruled him as a transitory wallow in a warm bath of illusion. His own way of life, where each knew his place, seemed infinitely preferable to the chaos of these freebooters who happened to rule him. So the Hindus paid their taxes, worshipped their gods, retained their idols, revered their Brahmins – and endured.

But not to change is to stagnate. Hinduism had progressed from the Vedas to the Upanishads to the philosophers. Now nothing new happened at all. Hinduism

A group of Indian ascetics, including Hindu and Mohammedan mystics.
British Museum.

had retired into its castle and pulled up the drawbridge. New things were dangerous, like the itinerant merchant who is allowed into the castle but turns out to be an enemy spy.

Moslem and Hindu grew apart until now they are so far apart they live, save for a minority, in separate countries. At only one time in the history of Moslem rule did it seem that they might come together. Most of the Moguls were bigots. One, Akbar, was not. Having made himself a vast empire, he decided that he did not know which of all the religions was truly the religion of God. He arranged disputations between Hindu and Moslem divines, to which he listened attentively. He even sent to the West for some Christians to join the fray. Two Jesuits made the journey. They were shown into the presence of the Great Moghul, and gave him a present. It was a copy of the Bible. Akbar put it on his head. Overjoyed, the Jesuits foresaw his conversion. Unfortunately for them, the gesture was mere politeness: there was little else Akbar could do with a book, because he could not read.

Akbar was converted neither to Hinduism, nor to Christianity. While he was puzzling over who was the true God, a solution suddenly hit him. *He* was God. He prepared to announce this to the wide world, but the Moslem divines, thoroughly alarmed, persuaded him to drop the notion.

The English replaced the Moslems. It should be remembered that they were not the almost pagan English of today. Every man was a Christian, and it was a Christian's duty to wash the heathen in the blood of the Lamb. Missionaries were sent out to India, only to find that Christians of St Thomas had existed in India centuries before England had ever heard of the faith. The English eagerly brought the Good News, only to find it was no news at all. The Hindus treated them with indifference, at which the missionaries began to direct their preaching in the wrong direction. The point of conquering India (which cost money) was to get some money back, by fair means or foul. The missionaries, observing the second category, began to try and convert the English administrators into honest men, at which they lost all prestige and influence, never to regain it. Hinduism was once more safe.

Two conquests, however, had not left it quite unscathed. It had defended itself by rigid orthodoxy, but orthodoxy is dull. Oppressed in the world at large, weighed down by ritual, many Hindus turned to that more emotional side of their religion, which had its roots deep in Tantrism. Bhakti Yoga, the path of devotion, increased its following and its fervour. Worship through sexual acts drew more and more followers. The missionaries were horrified, but failed to drum up much interest in it at home, partly because it was not a thing that could be

Jesuits debating with Moslem divines before the Emperor Akbar.
Miniature by Nan Sing from a manuscript of Abu Fazl's Akbar-Nama,
1602–6. Chester Beatty Library, Dublin.

explained by lantern slides. The English administrators regarded it with amused detachment, merely warning their wives that the natives were not nice people.

One sect they did take notice of: I must mention them here, because the idea of Hindu mysticism can still conjure up in the West visions of the Thugs. The Thugs (or more correctly Thags) were worshippers of the goddess Bhavani, a form of the goddess Kali, whose major delights were blood and dancing on the prostrate form of her husband, Siva. The Thugs were also robbers, but it would be rash to treat them as mere thieves around whom legends have collected. They were men who were dedicated to killing at random on behalf of an idea. They may be classed with modern terrorists who spread death among innocent people. In the case of the moderns, it is for a political idea; in the case of the Thugs, it was for religion.

Their method of execution was to slowly garrot the victim by means of a noose, praying to Bhavani in between the jerks. This, at least, is the way that took the West's fancy, although the Thugs used other means of killing. The sect spread. Normally, the English administration did not interfere with any aspect of religion. But the Thugs were a menace to the two deities of the administration: Law and Order. Campaigns were mounted against them, and they were destroyed.

They were a minor scourge, but they received enormous publicity. In the snug, safe Western world of the late nineteenth century, it was deliciously frightening to think that, while you were walking quietly on the street, someone could come up behind you and strangle you. A New Yorker today would think it commonplace, but for the Victorian it was bizarre. For a long time the Hindu religion was tarred with this brush: Indian gentlemen, quietly studying for a law degree in London, were considered capable of committing murder at the behest of the goddess. A highly successful melodrama, *The Green Goddess*, written by an otherwise intelligent drama critic, only added to the picture.

This, echoing back from the West, caused many thoughtful Indians to examine the true state of Hinduism. They found it had ossified. There were many things in it of which they could rightly be ashamed. The caste system, which led to the cruel repression of the Untouchable, was something no Western-educated Hindu could pass by: child-marriage was another. On a philosophical plane, the teachings of the Upanishads had been buried under a mass of superstitions. From the notion of God as Self, Hinduism had degenerated into something not far short of pure idolatory.

A movement, started by Westernized Indians, was organized to reform the faith. It was known as 'Brahmo Samaj'. It was never very successful, but it directed attention once more to the Upanishads, and the gurus and swamis who tour the world today owe much to its initiative.

A contemplative swami: only the flowing hair indicates that he is putting the world behind him in old age, as required by Vedanta.

Some sincere swamis never gather a following. The little crowd around this man with his home-made public address system is gathered to watch the photographer, not him.

This swami looks perhaps like the original sages of the Upanishads:
his hair is dyed green.

In spite of the Hindu–Moslem rift which resulted from the Moslem conquest of India,
examples of peaceful cohabitation exist. Here, in Srinagar (Kashmir), is a shrine to
Kali (see also colour plate, p. 180) on the wall of the Shahi-Hamdan mosque,
respected by members of both faiths. >

Ramakrishna

The members of the Brahmo Samaj had praiseworthy aims. They wanted to reform the Hindu religion so that its believers could hold up their heads in front of the world, and particularly in front of the English. They wished to abolish the marriage of children: they wanted to abolish the caste system: they wished to do away with idols. They were high-minded and right-minded. Such people are admirable, but they do not often change history.

They believed in meditation, but meditation on God. Naturally, given their respect for the opinions of the English, this god was not the neutral space within the heart, but a personal god: this god was stripped of the attributes that Hinduism had heaped on Siva, Brahma and Vishnu. He did not have six arms and three heads. In truth, he was no more Hindu than the Archbishop of Canterbury.

One group met regularly in Calcutta to meditate upon this god. In their midst was often a man in a loincloth, bare-chested, with a stubbly beard. He had the looks and figure of a peasant, and he spoke with a peasant's dialect. The other members of the group were gentlemen born, but they treated the remarks of this half-clad man with respect. The remarks were always wise, and sometimes delightful.

One day this peasant had joined in a group meditation on god. When it was over, and when he had left, he said to one of his companions: 'I've just seen a lot of you meditating, and do you know what it reminded me of? Troops of monkeys sometimes sit quietly under the trees of Dakshineswar [where the speaker lived], just as if they were perfect gentlemen, quite innocent. But they aren't. They're sitting there thinking about all those gourds and pumpkins that householders train to grow over their roofs, and about all the gardens full of plaintains and eggplants. After a little while, they'll jump up with a yell and rush away to stuff their stomachs. I saw many of you meditating like that.'

Ramakrishna: a statue in an Indian branch of the Ramakrishna Mission.

The listening Brahmo Samajists laughed. The peasant often did make people laugh: sometimes at him, but more times with him. He was Ramakrishna, clown, play-actor, transvestite, madman, and a saint, one of the most authentic saints in all Hinduism. It was he, and not the Brahmo Samajists, who changed history.

He was born in 1836 in a small village. His parents were modest farmers, but there was, so to speak, religion in the family: an elder brother was chief priest in the temple of the goddess Kali, at Dakshineswar in the big city of Calcutta. Needless to say, the priest was a Brahmin and so were all the family.

Little Gadahar Chattopadhyaya (for that was Ramakrishna's real name) was a charming boy, full of high spirits and gaiety. At the age of seven he became subject to epileptic fits. His whole body would grow rigid and he would stay for long periods in a state of trance. Since these fits came on most frequently at religious ceremonies, the villagers treated them as an asset rather than otherwise, and all predicted a religious career for him.

One day he carried things a little too far. A festival in honour of Siva was to be held. Part of it was the open-air performance of a play that narrated incidents from the mythology of the god, the actors being, as was the custom, all boys. On the day of the festival the boy who was to play Siva fell ill. It was decided that Gadahar should play the part. He protested at this, but he was overruled. He was made up to represent the god as a monk, Siva's favourite disguise. He approached the stage with a preternatural dignity that awed the audience. He had an expression of deep abstraction on his face, very proper for a god. He mounted the stage, and stood still. The audience fell into a deep silence. He went on standing still. The audience began to grow restive. The boy still did not move a muscle. The audience began to shout at him. They advised various ways of making him get on with the entertainment, including throwing cold water at him. Nothing, however, could make him move. The play, now ruined, was stopped and little Gadahar was carried off, still rigid. He did not come out of his fit for many hours.

It was decided that the best thing for him was to follow in his brother's footsteps and become a priest. He served under his brother in the temple of Kali, but once again he carried things too far. He developed an exaggerated devotion to the image of the goddess. He meditated for long hours in front of it, praying passionately, sometimes in floods of tears, that the idol should come to life. He addressed Kali as Mother and cried out like a child for Mother to come to him.

All this was embarrassing for the other priests, and particularly for his brother, who felt a family responsibility for the scenes, disturbing as they did the quiet, orderly ritual prescribed by the sacred texts. Opinion was divided about the cause of it all; some said the boy was insane, others that he was merely dotty.

Matters came to a head when he proclaimed that Kali – Mother – had really come to him in a vision. This gave weight to the opinion of those who thought him mad, and he was fired from his post.

Now followed twelve years of wandering in the forest, praying, and practising asceticism. As in all these preparatory periods in the lives of the saints of any religion, we cannot trust the evidence too firmly. The saint is alone, and where there is little known, legends grow. It seems, however, on his own evidence, that Gadahar, now a man, met a nun, wandering like himself, who initiated him into the Tantric sex rites that we have briefly described. He, in later life, said that he had only escaped moral depravity because Mother had come to his assistance. He made a balanced comment on this period. The orthodox Hindu has always held that much of Tantrism was merely moral turpitude, and hateful. When one such person had expressed his opinion to the saint, he replied: 'Why do you give way to hatred? I tell you, this is also one of the paths, though a dirty one. There are several doors leading into a house – the main door, the door by which the sweeper enters to clean out the dirt. So this, too, is a door. No matter which door people use, they get inside the house all right. Does that mean you should act with them, or mix with them? No – but keep your heart free of hatred for them.'

This sober and wise judgment comes from his maturity, and gives an impression of a mellowed sage. He was never that, or at least, never mellow for more than a few minutes. So far as Tantrism is concerned, his position is clear. With that sublime illogicality of parents, his father and mother had decided, when he still held down his job in the temple, that the cure for his craziness was that he should get married. A child bride was found for him. Gadahar seemed pleased with the idea. He stayed married to her all his life. But even when she came to the age when it was thought proper for a husband to have sexual relations with her, he refused, and went on refusing. His marriage was perfectly chaste.

Having escaped from the wandering nun, he returned to Dakshineswar, where he met a monk who spent most of his life totally naked. This man had only two possessions: some tongs for making a fire, and a waterpot. He belonged to a sect of monks, also nude, who held firmly to the teachings of the Upanishads.

Meeting Gadahar, he asked him abruptly if he wished to be taught the Vedanta. Gadahar replied with perfect simplicity, 'I don't know, it all depends on Mother. If she says "Yes", then I'll do it.'

The monk replied, 'All right. Go and ask your mother,' thinking that a young man sought a real mother's permission, as young men in India do. Gadahar went, not to his house, but to the Kali temple. He came out beaming with joy. 'Mother says yes,' he said, '"Go and learn. That monk came here specially to teach you".'

This was not at all pleasing to the monk, who was called Tota. To him the temple, the idol, Kali and visions were all claptrap and mummery: he was a staunch and true follower of the rebels. But he was moved by Gadahar's innocence, so he decided to teach him. But first Gadahar must give up being a Brahmin. This was an extraordinary sacrifice to ask, equal to asking a prince of the blood royal to give up his title and his claim to the throne. Gadahar agreed: whether out of his innocence, or because Mother told him, or because he already felt deep within him his mission in the world – we cannot say. Two hours before the dawn, in a hut which still exists, Gadahar had his Brahminical thread taken away, and his topknot shorn off. Tota gave him a new name, Ramakrishna. That, too, like the hut, was to last to our times, one of the most honoured names in India.

Ramakrishna was now, it is to be presumed, a convinced non-dualist, as the Indian philosophers called it: that is to say, he no longer believed that there was a worshipper and something to be worshipped. Both were contained in one – the real self. Non-dualism was opposed by dualism, God worshipped by man. The conversion was spectacular. Few people have ever been such enthusiastic worshippers of a separate deity as Ramakrishna, as the following instance shows.

On one occasion he was seized with a desire to worship the god Krishna. Krishna, as we have seen, had enjoyed dalliance with woman, so what could be more logical than that Ramakrishna (or Gadahar, as he still was) should approach his god as a female. He set about the business with his usual intensity. A rich admirer gave him the necessary clothes – an expensive sari from Benares, a skirt and a bodice. With this went a wig and jewellery. Once in these he studied how to walk like a woman, speak like one, and use female gestures, which, in India, are much more delicate than those of a male. Having perfected the impersonation, he visited some women friends and they could not believe that he was a man. Not satisfied with this, he dressed and did the hair of the wife of a friend, gave her wise instructions on the art of femininity, and then led her to her husband. Those who already thought him mad, now thought him perverted. He brushed this calumny aside. He was, he maintained, quite sincerely a woman.

At any rate, he was so successful in his aim that, worshipping Krishna, he saw a vision of the god. When this disappeared, he was heartbroken, weeping and refusing food, like a girl abandoned by her lover.

His attention turned to another god, Rama. Rama had, it was narrated, made war on a demon. In this he was greatly helped by a miraculous monkey called Hanuman. Ramakrishna decided to worship Rama in the guise of the monkey. Dress was scarcely adequate for this. We have a description of what he did, in his own words:

'I had to walk like Hanuman, I had to eat like him, and do every action as he would have done it. I didn't do this of my own accord: it happened of itself. I tied my dhoti [loincloth] round my waist to make it look like a tail, and I moved about in jumps. I ate nothing but fruit and nuts, and I didn't like them when they were skinned or peeled. I spent a lot of my time in trees, and I kept crying "Rama" in a deep voice. My eyes got a restless look like the eyes of a monkey. And the most marvellous thing was – the lower end of my spine lengthened, nearly an inch! Later, when I stopped practising this kind of devotion, it gradually went back to its normal size.'

We may regard the nascent tail as the playfulness of a born story-teller. But his utter sincerity shines through in one phrase, 'I didn't do this of my own accord: it happened of itself.' Every parent will know that it is useless to ask a child *why* he is Tarzan, or a pirate, or an astronaut. It just happens that he is. Observers of Ramakrishna, even those who were hostile, all agree that he never lost contact with his childhood. It is a great gift. It is said that when a genius dies, there is a little boy, looking just as he was when he was young, to take him by the hand and lead him gently across the line. I hope it happened to Ramakrishna.

While he did not see Rama (or it is not recorded that he did), he had a vision of Sita, Rama's wife. She was an exceedingly beautiful woman, and Ramakrishna saw her with his eyes open, the first vision, he tells us, that he had without shutting his eyes. He fell unconscious to the ground, but not before Sita, with divine courtesy, had made him a present of her smile.

His visions continued as he matured, but it is a little saddening to note they lost some of their innocence. They become more planned, and more didactic. There is a sense that he is trying too hard. For instance, at one period he became a Moslem. He dressed like a Moslem, he prayed to Allah five times a day as the Faith prescribes. 'I felt disinclined', he narrates, 'even to see images of the Hindu gods and goddesses, much less worship them – for the Hindu way of thinking had disappeared altogether from my mind. I spent three days in that mood.' At the end of them he had a vision of the Prophet.

The last of his visions has a touch of *déjà vu*. It is a little mechanical. Again a friend introduced him to a new faith. He read to him some passages of Sri Isha, the Hindu name for Jesus. Ramakrishna began to think about Sri Isha. He studied daily a picture of the Virgin Mary. Once again his devotion to the gods of Hinduism faded. This was replaced by visions 'of Christian priests burning incense and waving lights before images of Jesus in their churches.' Three days later he saw a tall, stately man with a fair complexion walking towards him. He was beautiful in spite of the fact that he had his nose 'slightly flattened at the tip'. A great voice sounded within him, saying, 'This is Jesus Christ, the great yogi, the loving Son of God and one with his Father, who shed his heart's blood and suffered tortures for the salvation of mankind.' Jesus then passed into Ramakrishna's body.

The Christian reader may reasonably doubt that the tall man with the pugilist's nose was really Jesus. The voice that Ramakrishna heard within may have misled him: it was certainly shaky in its syntax. And, after all, Christian priests do not wave lights in front of images. That is purely a Hindu form of devotion.

It was not so much his visions that drew people to him. It was his uniqueness as a man, his unpredictability, and his obvious sincerity, three qualities which later drew millions to Mahatma Gandhi.

As for his unpredictability, it kept his most faithful disciples with their hearts in their mouths. He took up quarters in the temple of Kali where he had once served, and there received a constant stream of visitors. One very important one came to visit him, only to find him chatting and cracking jokes with a dancing girl. Such a woman was considered a prostitute, for the good reason that she frequently was. The important visitor left in disgust, convinced that Ramakrishna had a mistress.

Ramakrishna was accustomed to wear only a dhoti. He was very fond of the theatre. Money was by this time pouring into the temple as a tribute to him. His administrator (of whom I shall speak below) arranged coins in neat piles in front of him so that he could reward the actors, a custom of the time. He was meant to be polite and give equally to all the performers. Ramakrishna would have none of it. Delighted by the performance of one woman, he thrust all the money at her, and she took it. Later, he wanted to reward another actor, but there was no money. So he took off his dhoti and gave him that.

His disregard for what he wore got him struck off Calcutta's social register. He had become a celebrity, and he was much sought after. Devendranath Tagore, the father of the famous poet, was a very prominent man in social circles. He extended an invitation to Ramakrishna to come and have a meal with him, something which was sure to raise the holy man's status. But Devendranath was also a stick; he believed the social niceties should be observed. He therefore asked Ramakrishna not to turn up naked to the waist, but to put on some more clothes. We have seen that Ramakrishna had no objections to dressing up in honour of a god. But Devendranath had not that status. Ramakrishna refused, saying he had no other clothes. Devendranath never asked him again.

He was, in any case, a disconcerting guest, or host. For no reason at all he would start singing songs in a sweet voice, or get up and start dancing by himself. He was very fond of a good, romping dance. Driving in a carriage one night, he saw some drunken men on the sidewalk dancing ring-a-roses. With a cry of delight, Ramakrishna leapt from his carriage and joined in the revels.

On the other hand, people who visited him expecting to find a child-like saint, full of sweetness and light, were in for a shock. There was nothing angelic in his face. It was lined and bearded, its peasant quality enhanced by his habit of wearing a rag twisted round his head, like a housewife's mob-cap. He spoke the rough dialect of his village, and could neither read nor write. He used obscene words quite freely, this being natural among villagers. This was mitigated by the fact that he spoke with an attractive stammer, but it managed to outrage quite a number of bourgeois who expected to see a saint who could be brought into the drawing-room.

His most marked characteristic was his habit of falling into a trance any time and anywhere. These trances, too, just 'happened'. There were no prolonged preparations, no hymn-singing, no chanting of mantras by disciples. He just dropped into a trance as one drops off into a nap in a tropical afternoon. As for Hatha Yoga and all its exercises, he would have nothing to do with it. A guru taught him some, but he pointed out, with perfect logic, that you cannot forget your body by spending hours twisting it about. As to the idea that doing this would give you occult powers, it made him angry. 'Shun them, like filthy excrement,' he said. 'Sometimes they come of themselves when you practise devotion. But if you take any notice of them, you'll stick fast. You won't be able to reach God.'

What did he mean by God? That he believed in gods is clear. He worshipped them as an Italian worships saints. That he saw these saints might also be accepted. The Virgin Mary is always appearing in Catholic countries, to the exasperation of the ecclesiastical authorities, who do not want a Lourdes in every village, for administrative reasons. Ramakrishna seemed much of the same opinion. In spite of his personal ecstasies, the god that he taught his disciples was that of the Upanishads, the real self. He solved the contradictions of this by simply making no attempt to do so – the mark of a perfectly genuine man.

He went further. He discouraged over-enthusiasm in others, especially when it came to his own teaching. Talking to his disciples one day, he advised them that one should not return evil for evil. But noticing that the young men round him were taking this pacific advice too literally, he told a story. His method of instruction often included parables and, since this was one of his best, it bears repeating.

There was once (he said) a cobra which gave a great deal of trouble to the boys who watched over a herd of cows, making sudden dashes at them, and frightening them out of their wits. A swami was walking one day across the cobra's territory. Instantly the snake reared its head, spread its hood (a sign that it meant to strike) and, arrow-like, made for the swami's feet. The swami intoned a spell. Instantly, the cobra lay flat on the ground, its hood collapsed. The swami gave the snake a little lecture on its bad habits. Then he said, 'From today onwards you will bite nobody. Now go your ways in peace.' The abashed snake slithered off.

The cobra, an earnest and religious soul, faithfully obeyed the swami's command. Since it could not kill small rodents, it struggled along on a diet of roots and grass. It grew weak and thin and slow. One day the cowherds saw it, dragging itself wearily along. They plucked up courage and seizing their sticks, beat it almost to death. The cobra, with a great effort, escaped them.

The next day, famished, it dragged itself out of its hole to find food, and met the swami. It feebly raised its head in greeting.

'But what is all this?' said the swami. 'What has happened? Why are you so thin and feeble?'

'Swami,' said the snake in a thread of a voice, 'I think that soon I shall be dead. I have killed nothing since the day I met you, and I have grown so weak that the cowherds attacked me with their sticks. But, swami, give me a blessing before I die, for I obeyed your command.'

The swami clicked his tongue impatiently.

'But why in the holy name of Siva didn't you frighten the boys off?'

'Swami,' said the snake, 'you told me to bite no one, and I obeyed your orders.'

'Yes,' said the swami, 'but at least you could have *hissed*.'

Then muttering a spell, with no great good grace, he healed him.

Pragmatical with others, a prey to sudden ecstasies himself, Ramakrishna's fame grew with the years. People flocked to listen to him. So great was the press of people that his peace had to be defended by a faithful servant. This man, Hriday Ram, handled all his appointments. Without the visitor going through Hriday, Ramakrishna could not be seen. Hriday, like all such, began to profit from his position. He took money from visitors, and it soon amounted to a large sum. It was a scandal: in the end, Ramakrishna had to send him away, although with great reluctance. 'After all,' said the saint, excusing him, 'with all the money he made, he was able to buy himself a farm.'

For a saint, he was always a very human being. He had no patience at all with the mystification and jiggery-pokery that had grown up around the Upanishads. As we have seen, he detested talk of supernatural powers that were supposed to be acquired by adepts at Hatha Yoga, and he himself worked no miracles. When he fell ill, he suffered, and said so.

His last illness was a cruel one. He had an exceptionally fine singing voice, which he loved to exercise. He developed a cancer in his throat which not only caused him severe pain, but occasionally made it impossible for him to eat or drink. This is perhaps the place to point out that nowhere is it said that meditation is a cure for bodily sickness, unless it is a result of mental strain. The saints and the teachers die, as we all die.

They sometimes have an added burden to bear when they are ill, that of devoted but bone-stupid followers. One such troubled Ramakrishna's last days. Ramakrishna one day groaned to him that he was in great pain from an unbearable burning in his throat. The disciple, full of himself, immediately decided that this was all play-acting to test his faith. He pointed out with alacrity that Ramakrishna could not be suffering because the real self did not feel pain. Ramakrishna groaned. The disciple repeated his philosophical argument. Ramakrishna groaned even louder. Finally the disciple burst out, 'I don't care *what* you say, you cannot be ill. For me you are an ocean of tranquillity.' To which Ramakrishna replied, with polished irony, 'Ah, this rascal has found me out.'

He died on 16 August 1886. His fame had spread throughout Bengal. It might never have crossed its frontiers, if it had not been for one of his disciples, a man as remarkable as Ramakrishna, but in a different way.

The bronze statue in Bombay of Vivekananda, the successor to Ramakrishna.

Vivekananda

The disciple was Narendranath Dutt: but he has a place in the history books of both the East and the West, so I shall use the name under which he is to be found in the indices – Vivekananda. He was born in 1863 to a middle-class family in Calcutta. He died, aged 38, in 1902, a hero of Indian India. But when it came to his education, his family had no thoughts of Indian India at all. The English were their masters and they greatly admired them, as did many other Bengalis of the time. Vivekananda was a youth of great charm and intelligence. He had a somewhat round face, made beautiful by large, expressive eyes, set wide apart in the manner that film directors look for in choosing an actor. He early showed signs of a sharp intellect, and his parents decided that he should have an English education. He was sent to a missionary college, where he graduated.

It was the age of what the English contemptuously called 'babus', educated Bengalis who spoke fluent English, mostly with a comic accent and uproariously funny mistakes in English idioms. Their instruction was superficial, for they were meant to supply the clerks and underlings of the administration. Vivekananda soon showed a characteristic that was to remain with him throughout his life – nothing he ever did was superficial. He, too, admired the English, but not as his masters. He was attracted to the intellectual giants of the time. He buried himself in the works of Herbert Spencer, and John Stuart Mill, neither of whom had much appeal to teachers in a missionary college. But they did not stop him reading them.

It is easy enough to stop reading them now. Spencer and Mill breathe an optimism about the human race which now seems as quaint as a bustle. They were both agnostics: their faith lay in the perfectability of mankind. Herbert Spencer pointed to the newly-discovered theory of evolution to prove that things got better and better all the time, man included. John Stuart Mill maintained that liberty was all that was needed to make a paradise on earth. We have no such heart-warming, upward-looking philosophers today, except, perhaps, the late

Teilhard de Chardin, the Jesuit who believed that we shall all end up one day as one single, progressive Mind. But even he was banned from publishing by his own Jesuit Order.

The young Vivekananda, however, was deeply impressed. Spencer and Mill gave him hope that Indians would one day struggle out of the apathy and torpor which he found all around him. Like all bright men in their late 'teens, he was interested in religion, but in a sceptical way. He joined the Brahmo Samaj, but did not find much satisfaction among those well-meaning but ineffectual gentlemen.

He visited Ramakrishna, naturally as a sceptic. His reception bowled him over. Ramakrishna fell in love with the young man. It was not a homosexual love, but it looked so much like it that the other disciples were uneasy. He held Vivekananda's hand, he gazed into his eyes, he took him off to a private verandah, and fed him sweetmeats with his own hand. Vivekananda was acutely embarrassed.

However, flattery is sweet to a very young man, and Vivekananda began to visit the saint. But not often enough for Ramakrishna. When he did visit, Ramakrishna would be bereft of speech at the sight of him and go into a trance. When he stayed away, Ramakrishna would weep, 'I can't bear it when I don't see him,' he would say to his disciples. 'I weep so much and still he doesn't come. He doesn't understand at all what I feel for him. What will people think seeing a man of my age weeping and pining for a boy like him? . . . And yet I can't stop myself.'

Ramakrishna was not really a man who cared much about what people thought, as can be seen from an incident at a Brahmo Samaj meeting which borders on the farcical. Ramakrishna attended the session as was his wont from time to time. Hymns were to be sung and Vivekananda was in the choir. Ramakrishna made his way to the altar, saw him, and instantly fell into a trance. The congregation, which was already standing on the benches to get a good look at the celebrated saint, now fell into utter confusion. The ushers tried to restore some order and decorum into what was intended to be a solemn religious service, but in vain. The ushers then hit upon the idea of turning out the lights to bring the meeting to an end. This resulted in a wild stampede for the doors. Meantime, Ramakrishna remained in his trance. Vivekananda, furious at being the cause of the chaos, pushed his way through the darkness and the throng, gathered up the still unconscious Ramakrishna, put him in a carriage and took him home.

When Ramakrishna had recovered his senses, the boy gave the saint a good wigging. But, as Vivekananda has recorded, Ramakrishna did not mind his scolding in the least: 'he was just happy to have me with him again. So then I spoke to him very severely: "It is written (I said) that King Bhavata thought so much about his favourite deer that he himself became a deer after his death. If that's true, you should beware of thinking so much about me." The Master [Vivekananda goes on] was as simple as a young boy. He took what I said literally, and asked me in great distress, "You are right – so what's going to happen to me since I can't bear not seeing you?" '

Apparently Ramakrishna decided that the idea of being reborn as the lad on whom he had set his heart was not too dreadful, for he continued to insist on seeing him. He tried to teach Vivekananda the principles of the Upanishads, but Vivekananda was once more up in arms. 'What is this nonsense about "I am God, you are God, everything that is born and dies is God",' said the boy. 'The authors of the Upanishads must have been mad – how else could they have written such stuff?' It did not help when Ramakrishna started quoting things his Mother (the goddess Kali, it will be recalled) had told him about Vivekananda, of whom, it seemed, she highly approved. Ramakrishna was convinced that Vivekananda was a great man (a familiar belief among men who dote on youngsters) and Mother agreed. Not so Vivekananda. He fell back on Herbert Spencer as a last defence.

'How do you *know*', he said, 'that it was Mother who told you? Science and philosophy tell us that our senses often deceive us, especially when there's a desire in our minds to believe something. You are fond of me and you want to believe I'm a great man – that may be why you have these visions.'

It is a striking picture: the doting old man face to face with the cool and rational youth putting him to rights. It turned out that the youth was wrong and the old man (not to mention Mother) was right. Vivekananda *was* a great man.

There were dangers to overcome first: he was being outrageously flattered by the most celebrated holy man in Bengal, as perilous a position as being the young favourite of a Renaissance Pope. He was what in Bengal was called 'a brilliant fellow', that is to say, a clever student with a quick grasp of books, a type that soon degenerates (in the words of another Bengali, N. C. Chaudheri) into a man who is well-versed in the titles on the spines of books. A boy who had formed his own ideas from reading the rationalists, he was being courted by a man of no education who was capable of saying, 'What is Logic? Explain it to me', and then changing the conversation after a few words.

He survived these perils because he was a young man of strong character; he needed, as do most people of that type, a nasty blow from fate to bring it out in him. It duly came.

He had spent his childhood and adolescence in comfortable circumstances. His father was a man of a generous and cheerful disposition. He believed that life was something to enjoy and not worry about. When he died, it was found that he had followed his philosophy so faithfully that he had left his family penniless and deep in debt. Vivekananda had to get a job, otherwise the family would not eat.

India, then and now, is a country where one can fall from comfort to destitution in a few days. There are no social security nets to break the fall. There is the family, a much-lauded institution in the land. An unfortunate relative would not be allowed, for shame, to beg on the streets. He would be taken in to do his begging, in the less public role of a poor relation. Pride and a sense of his own abilities made Vivekananda decide to be the mainstay of his family.

He went from office to office, from family friend to family friend, asking for work. Nobody would give him any. It was his first lesson in the web of studied indifference within which an Indian can retire when it comes to anything which touches opening his purse. It was a bitter one: he never forgave his countrymen, and lashed them with his tongue all his short life.

There is one point that the hagiographers of both Vivekananda and Ramakrishna never raise. At this time (as we have seen) Ramakrishna had achieved such celebrity that he could break up a meeting by his sheer presence. Why, then, did he not exert himself to find his favourite a job? He had by this time a wide acquaintance among the well-heeled: he himself and his disciples could not have survived without them. Was he afraid of being lonely when Vivekananda signed the book each morning to get behind his babu's desk? Or did he know, with the super-egoistical insight of the holy, that Vivekananda was the only one among his friends who would ensure his being remembered after he was dead?

I cannot say. All we have is an edifying and quite unconvincing story. Vivekananda did raise the point with his mentor. His family, he told him, were on the verge of starving. They needed immediate help. Ramakrishna told him to go pray to the Mother.

Vivekananda went into the temple. Three times he began a prayer to ask help for his family from the goddess. Three times he could not finish it properly. All he could ask was for Knowledge of the Truth for himself.

I don't believe a word of it. In the first place, Ramakrishna was face to face with a fiery-tempered Bengali youth, forced, despite his natural pride, to ask urgent help from a man who had embarrassingly pressed his attentions on him. If Ramakrishna had brushed him off with a curt advice to pray, he would have got, I fancy, a reply which would have sent him off into another of his public trances. Secondly, while Vivekananda might well have prayed to Kali in his troubles (he had been on his knees in a dozen houses already), he would not have switched to a pretty-please prayer for himself. All his life poverty horrified him. He himself said that it caused him to have a bleeding heart, and there was no irony in his use of the phrase, whatever may have happened to it since.

Things were smoothed over. The family were looked after and we hear no more of them. Vivekananda did not have to get a job: he was free to join Rama-krishna's growing community of devotees. We may assume that some monied patron saw to it that the saint should be happy. As for Ramakrishna, we have his lapidary phrase about such things: 'Religion', he once said, 'is not made for empty bellies'.

From now on Vivekananda dropped the doubts and hostilities which had hitherto been a barrier between the two men. Ramakrishna relied on his friend's overt abilities more and more, putting him into the position of a sort of head-master over the other disciples. Vivekananda, for his part, learned to ignore the wilder gyrations of the saint's personality, to attend with respect to his message, and to value his continuing love. After Ramakrishna's death, he never ceased to say that all his ideas came from his Master, though others who had sat at the same Master's feet said that emphatically they did not.

The additions he made to Ramakrishna's gospel were due to an experience which the saint had never ventured upon. When Ramakrishna died, Vive-kananda went on a pilgrimage, which took him the length and breadth of India. At times he was entertained by rajas: at others he changed his name and travelled as a mendicant sadhu. He was in a spiritual turmoil. A man now inevitably dedicated to religion, he had been taught that it was a thing not meant for the hungry. But millions of Indians all around him were hungry: millions lived in squalor: millions of the well-off were too lazy to give a damn about it.

It had been noticed before. The English blamed it on the Indians, saying they were hidebound by caste, slothful by choice, and selfish. The Indians blamed it on the English, saying they were hard-hearted by race, grasping by policy, and had their eyes always fixed on Home, which was the British Isles. Vivekananda tramped the country, sat on a rock at Cape Comorin at the southernmost tip of the Indian peninsula, and decided to blame it on the Hindu religion.

He returned on his steps with a jolting message. There are a great number of leading Indians who today (the 1970s) are saying the same thing, so his words are worth quoting. He attacks the endless Indian claim that Indians are superior to Westerners because they possess 'spiritual depths' which the West lacks.

We talk foolishly against material civilization. The grapes are sour. Even taking all that foolishness for granted, in all India there are, say, a hundred thousand really spiritual men and women. Now, for the spiritualization of these, must three hundred million be sunk in savagery and starvation? Why should they starve? How was it possible for the Hindu to have been conquered by the Moslems? It was due to the Hindus' ignorance of material civilization. . . . Material civilization, nay, even luxury, is necessary to create work for the poor.

Bread! Bread! I do not believe that a God who cannot give me bread here can give me eternal bliss in heaven! Pooh! India is to be raised, the poor are to be fed, education is to be spread, and the evil of priest-craft is to be removed. No priest-craft, no social tyranny! More bread! More opportunity for everybody. . . . Root up priest-craft from the old religion and you get the best religion in the world.

So we are back to the Brahmins and the rebel sages. The best religion in the world was that of the Upanishads, or the Vedanta, as its later development was called. Vivekananda, remembering the lessons of his Master, began to preach Vedanta with all his magnificant vocal resources.

It was now 1893. A Universal Exposition was being held at Chicago. It was one of the earliest of these things and far more effective than its successors. We owe our pillared banks and colonnaded town halls to the neo-classical style which it popularized. It was the apotheosis of material progress. But America was still, at that time, a religious country. All religions being tolerated, the more spiritually minded citizens decided to have a Parliament of Religions in Chicago at the same time. Then if God and Mammon were not to have exactly equal time, the Parliament would at least make sure that God had a hearing.

One of Vivekananda's admirers was the Raja of Ramnad. He decided to send Vivekananda to the Parliament as the representative of Hinduism. It was a little like sending a Luther to represent the Roman Catholic faith, but that did not matter, since the Americans knew nothing whatever of the Hindu faith and few had ever seen an Indian. The Raja raised the cash and, with considerable prescience, Vivekananda's costume. This consisted of a long red robe, drawn in at the waist by an orange cord, the whole topped with a great yellow turban. This represented no actual Indian dress, ecclesiastical or lay, but it had the advantage of overcoming Vivekananda's one disability. He had a resonant voice, an enviable flow of words, and a mastery of English: he was, however, only of medium height. The long robe and the high turban made him look imposing.

He arrived in Chicago in July and went to the Exhibition. He was as astonished as a child, and well he might be. The Raja and he knew so little about America that he went there without any credentials, or even the address of the organizers of the Parliament. Why should he need them? In India he merely arrived in a town, stopped the first passer-by and every Hindu door would be open to him. None of this worried him for a few days: he was so astonished and delighted by the New World. Like other Indians of those times he had no sense of urgency. He wandered, entranced. Not only the Universal Exposition had been designed to entertain: so, for Vivekananda, had Chicago and all its inhabitants.

Then he bethought him of enquiring about the Parliament. He went to the information office of the Exposition. He was told that the Parliament would meet in September. He was not on the list of delegates, for the good reason that nobody had written from India to say that he was coming. Nor could he get on the list without credentials. When he heard this, a sense of urgency hit him with a vengeance. Nobody in India, again, had troubled to calculate his expenses. His money was fast running out. He cabled to a religious society in Madras, but got a dusty answer. Indians travelling abroad in those days were regarded with suspicion. It was clear to those in Madras where the money had gone – in gorging on beef and making love to loose women. Gandhi, a few years before, had been thrown out of his caste for going to England; his struggles against the demon beef are narrated at length in his autobiography.

Vivekananda was down to his last few dollars. Somebody told him that Boston was a cheaper place to live in. He took train, and in it met a lady from Massachusetts. She took him home. There he met a fairy godmother in the unlikely guise of a Harvard professor. The professor gave him money and sent him back to Chicago with a letter of recommendation' to the Secretary of the coming Parliament.

All should have been well, but Vivekananda lost the address of the Secretary. Exactly as though he was in an Indian village, he stopped passers-by and asked them. With one glance at his bizarre attire, they fled. The Secretary was to have found him lodgings. Night came on, and again as though he were back in India, he curled up on a large box which he found in the railway station yard, and went soundly to sleep.

When he woke up, it was quite obvious to him what he should do. He was a travelling holy man, so, winding on his enormous turban, he went down the street, knocking at front doors, asking for charity. Housewives, seeing the turban, squealed with fright and slammed doors. Servants pushed him down front-steps and swore at him. The dogged swami persisted – he still liked America.

His devotion was rewarded. A woman, Mrs Hale, looking through her lace curtains, divined from the turban and robe that he was a delegate to the Parliament. No doubt Mother had a hand in this, because to most people he must have looked as though he was a mahout from Barnum and Bailey's circus.

Finding that he was indeed the actual, living, Hindu delegate, Mrs Hale carried him off to friends with all the enthusiasm of an American hostess who has captured a lion. He was lodged with the other delegates, credentials were given him, and all was well. He also landed his first American disciple – Mrs Hale.

The Parliament opened on 11 September. The principal delegates sat in a semicircle on the platform. In the centre was a Cardinal. Cardinals, with their purple silk, white lace, and huge pectoral cross, know how to dress for these occasions. But everybody in Chicago had seen a Cardinal's plumage. Nobody had seen a red robe topped by an enormous turban. In fact, it is probable that nobody had seen an East Indian. The Cardinal was eclipsed.

The delegates spoke. One thing had to be faced in such a meeting: so far as the Christians were concerned everybody would have heard everything before. There was not even a bit of wrangling from the floor to be hoped for; the aim of the Parliament was heavily ecumenical. But, on the other hand, the Hindu was a novelty. He was spanking new and that is what Americans have always loved. While the other delegates spoke, all eyes were on the turban. It had even been applauded when he entered.

Vivekananda rose. In his magnificent voice, sweeping the audience with his equally magnificent eyes, he spoke of Vedanta. He more than lived up to his turban. He spoke impromptu, but he was sure of himself. His simple, touching opening sentence was, 'Sisters and brothers of America!' It brought the house down. He spoke on the theme, 'All men are struggling through paths which in the end lead to Me.' The audience thought that this meant God. Only much later did they understand that Me meant themselves. As a subsequent American listener used to say, slapping his bald head: 'It amounted to this: the Absolute is Me.' However much or little they understood, they gave him a great ovation at the end of his discourse.

In all, he addressed the Parliament eleven times. Without him the Parliament would have been a flop. The audience rapidly got bored with the others. The alert reporter of the *Boston Evening Transcript* noted that the only way to keep the audience in their seats was to announce that Vivekananda would speak at the end of the meeting. Summing up the Parliament, the *New York Herald* said that he was undoubtedly the greatest figure in it. The paper added that it would be foolish to send missionaries to so learned a nation.

This understandably annoyed the Christian missionaries. They vigorously attacked Vivekananda. A group of Western intellectuals in India who had been unsuccessfully trying to raise American interest in Eastern religions were also incensed at having their thunder stolen before they had even achieved a preliminary rumble. They also attacked him, all of which, of course, only served to confirm that he was the most famous man of the hour.

Then, this being America, money began to pour in. It came in such quantities that it produced a nervous crisis in the famous young man. He really should not have been so surprised. In the middle of his discourses to the Parliament, he had inserted one with the title *Religion Not the Crying Need of India*, in which he appealed for those of his countrymen who were dying of hunger. When the cash came in, he rolled in agony on the floor saying, 'What have I to do with fame when people are lying in misery?' The answer would seem to be patent, namely to take the cash and post it off to those dying of hunger. But on sober reflection Vivekananda decided to use it, in this first instance, to finance his mission to the Americans. He arranged with a lecture agency for a wide tour of the States.

Lecture tours arranged by agencies can be very trying on the nerves. On occasions Vivekananda lost his temper. He surveyed the audience in Boston, did not like what he saw, and called them foxes and wolves. The audience began to disperse while he was still speaking. It is hard to imagine that anybody had called distinguished Bostonians foxes and wolves before, and to be called such names by a man with a yellow towel round his head was an outrage to propriety. The newspapers howled at his heels.

Matters did not improve when he attacked American Christianity. He proclaimed, 'It is all hypocrisy in this country! All this prosperity! All *this* from *Christ*! Christ would not find a stone to lay his head upon among you.'

This was offensive. A committee of clergymen got together and decided to investigate this strangely garbed Savonarola from the East (for Vivekananda's tirade was a quotation from the Florentine monk). They accused him of seducing a maidservant to the Governor of Michigan, which the Governor's wife had publicly to deny. To add to his troubles, orthodox Hindus from India accused him of not being a true Hindu and of betraying his religion. They said he ate beef with infidels. Vivekananda's reply gives us a good glimpse of the man. 'Do you mean to say', he wrote in reply, 'that I am born to live and die one of those caste-ridden, superstitious, merciless, hypocritical, atheistic cowards that you only find among the Hindus?' No, he answers himself, with considerable vehemence.

The well-heeled among his American admirers saw that this wild spirit would have to be tamed, and not only tamed but taught to wash behind his ears. He had no sense of money, but the way to teach him that was to give him plenty with, of course, strings. The social side was more difficult. America had no Kings or Queens or Maharajahs, or Viceroys. But it did have its Brahmins. Vivekananda was preaching compellingly about God, it was true. Yet if the Lodges spoke only to the Cabots and the Cabots spoke only to God, then the Cabots would probably know a thing or two about Him that had escaped the swami, who clearly had not hitherto moved in polished circles.

Rich Bostonians, rich New Yorkers therefore offered to give him ample finances, provided he would agree to associate only with the 'right' people. A touch of Vedanta could become what is today called a status symbol, but which was then described as 'refinement'. There had been other new religions, for example Spiritualism. But that had declined: even servants went to seances. Vedanta should be more aloof, more exclusive, and so should Vivekananda.

To his great credit (and to the shame of some of the swamis who came after him), Vivekananda turned down this offer with contempt. It was not that he did not want money. He wanted lots of it. He had already formed a plan. India was to provide the U.S. with the spiritual guidance it badly needed. America, in return, was to provide India with three hundred million rupees to banish its poverty. It was a modest proposal: it worked out at only a rupee a head. In today's money it was in the region of thirty million dollars. At the time, Americans thought Vivekananda had bats in his turban. They did not understand that the swami, with the simplicity of a child and the vision of a genius, had foreseen exactly what America would have to do, and is doing today all over the world. Nor are they getting free spirituality in return: they are having to pay for that too.

Vivekananda broke away from the rich and the 'right'. With the aid of some genuine but far from rich friends, he hired a room in New York at 64 West 33rd St. It was an unsalubrious neighbourhood, but people came to hear him in such numbers that they had to sit on the stairs outside. In the summer he taught at a country estate in Thousand Island Park, on the St Lawrence River. He visited England. He caused no great stir, the English having seen a considerable number of turbans. They treated him with kindness and respect as they did every educated Indian. As for Vivekananda, he admired them even more than he did the Americans. He was struck by the way they were taught at school to control their emotions; not, for instance, to roll on the floor when they had a problem. That this image was deliberately constructed in the Public Schools to turn out men who could awe the 'natives' does not seem to have occurred to him.

It was time, he now felt, to return to India. He made a leisurely journey through Europe, partly to restore his health. He was tired and he was depressed. He considered his mission a failure since he had not got the three hundred million rupees he wanted to relieve the misery of his fellow-countrymen. He saw that he would have to go on working and he viewed the prospect of endless lecturing with a horror that is human and touching.

He got back to India. His reception there was so overwhelming that, for a while, his vigour was restored. Crowds lined the quay as his ship berthed. Processions with drums and banners were organized everywhere in his honour. Any doubts the orthodox had about him were drowned in the general enthusiasm. He had gained world-wide fame: he was an Indian. That was enough for the common man to throw his hat in the air and swell with pride in him, whether he had eaten beef or not. Proudest of all was the Raja who had sent him to America and who had designed the turban and the robe. Obviously a man of artistic sensibility, he welcomed his protégé with a sumptuous cortège and a choir singing choruses from Handel.

The only people who did not exactly jump for joy were his old companions, the disciples of Ramakrishna. He might have been expected to return and take Ramakrishna's place, preaching the dead saint's gentle gospel. He returned, but, to the disciples' astonishment, set about giving all Hindu holy men a thorough lambasting. He wanted instead, he told them, Western ideas of action, service, organization, and once again, action, *action*. When one of the disciples remarked mildly that this was scarcely what their common Master, Ramakrishna, had taught, Vivekananda rounded on him.

'What do you know?' he roared at him, 'You are an ignorant man.' Then, turning to the rest of the flabbergasted disciples, he went on, 'You are sentimental fools! What do you understand of religion? You are only good for praying with folded hands, "O Lord! How beautiful is Your nose! How sweet are Your eyes!" and all such nonsense. You think your salvation is secured and Shri Ramakrishna will come at the final hour and take you by the hand to the highest heaven. According to you, study, public preaching, and doing humanitarian works are illusions because he said to someone "Seek and find God first: doing good in the world is a presumption!" As if God is such an easy thing to be achieved!' And turning to the original disciple who had occasioned this outburst, he ended cuttingly, 'As if He is such a fool as to make Himself a plaything in the hands of an imbecile.'

Later he declared himself even more bluntly. 'Who cares for your Scriptures? I will go into a thousand hells cheerfully, if I can arouse my countrymen to stand on their own feet and be MEN inspired with the spirit of action.'

This was the beginning of the Ramakrishna Mission that he founded, and which flourishes today. The disciples were to go out into the land. They were to do humanitarian work: heal the sick, work with their hands even to the extent of digging latrines. He demanded physical fitness.

'I want sappers and miners in the army of religion,' he said. 'So, boys, set yourself the task of training your muscles. For ascetics mortification is all right.

For workers, well-developed bodies, muscles of iron and nerves of steel!'

Once more he toured the country, ablaze with his passion for work. Everywhere he poured out his own immense forces to rouse Indians from the lethargy into which they had fallen after centuries of domination. 'The older I grow', he said 'the more everything seems to me to be in manliness: this is my new Gospel.'

Good works need money as well as muscle. Vivekananda, thinner now, and showing signs of illness, set out a second time for America. It was on this voyage that one of the most extraordinary incidents of his extraordinary life took place. Corsica is the birthplace of Napoleon Bonaparte. When Vivekananda's boat was off the island, he held a celebration. It was intended to express his disgust at the supine pacifism of the Indians. The celebration was in honour of Napoleon, 'The Lord of War'.

His reception in America was greater than ever, as well it might be, because his new Gospel was that of the Americans themselves. For all that, he felt depressed about America's future. It would not be, he felt, as glorious as he had once thought. In a strange moment of prophetic vision, he told a disciple, Sister Christine, 'The next upheaval that is to usher in another era, will come from Russia or from China. I cannot see clearly which, but it will be either one or the other.' This was said in 1896.

After another tour through Europe, he returned to India. He was very tired, and very sick with diabetes. On 4 July 1902 he died, his spirit and his body utterly worn out.

A great bronze monument has been erected to him in Bombay, at the Gateway of India. Plaques set around it give extracts from his speeches. One of his rallying cries was, 'Indians, get off your backsides.' It is not there. A large number of Indians today think that it should be. It still applies.

YE ARE THE CHILDREN OF GOD, THE SHARERS OF IMMORTAL BLISS, HOLY AND PERFECT BEINGS. YE DIVINITIES ON EARTH SINNERS! IT IS A SIN TO CALL A MAN SO; IT IS A STANDING LIBEL ON HUMAN NATURE. COME UP, O LIONS, AND SHAKE OFF THE DELUSION THAT YOU ARE SHEEP; YOU ARE SOULS IMMORTAL, SPIRITS FREE BLEST AND ETERNAL.

SWAMI VIVEKANANDA

INDIA WILL BE RAISED, NOT WITH POWER OF THE FLESH BUT WITH THE POWER OF THE SPIRIT NOT WITH THE FLAG OF DESTRUCTION, BUT WITH THE FLAG OF PEACE AND LOVE.... ONE VISION I SEE CLEAR AS LIFE BEFORE ME, THAT THE ANCIENT MOTHER HAS AWAKENED ONCE MORE, SITTING ON HER THRONE REJUVENATED, MORE GLORIOUS THAN EVER PROCLAIM HER TO ALL THE WORLD WITH THE VOICE OF PEACE AND BENEDICTION

SWAMI VIVEKANANDA

Quotations from Vivekananda at the base of his statue in Bombay (see page 136).

The doldrums

After Vivekananda's death, the Indians remained as firmly on their backsides as his statue remains on its base. Most of them, at least. A handful took his advice in such a way that, had he known about it, his ashes would have risen in a mushroom cloud. Vivekananda had not achieved the thirty million dollars that he wanted from the Americans. On the other hand, they had been generous to him. Thoughtful observers in India noted that he had made money. Those thoughtful observers took his advice, got off their posteriors and made for the States, the new Golconda.

Swamis, gurus and sadhus descended on America by the dozen. They had none of their predecessor's magnetism, nor his superb voice and presence. They could not expect to make much money by lecturing on the Vedanta. There was, however, something much more lucrative to hand and that was Hatha Yoga.

The trouble with the Upanishads was that when a student finally could say, like the bald-headed man, 'I am the Absolute', the question arose, 'Then what?' This new contingent of swamis assessed Americans with considerable shrewdness. It was a pragmatical society, devoted to business. Americans appreciated a tranquil mind, but they were inclined to believe that nothing was quite so soothing as a million dollars in the bank. Had not Vivekananda himself preferred muscles to meditation?

The Americans, like the British from whom they derived their culture, were devoted to physical exercise. An hour of Hatha Yoga was as invigorating as an hour in the gymnasium or a round of golf. But not *more* invigorating: besides, since it had to be practised alone, it lacked the possibility of making business contacts. The swamis needed an extra touch.

It was easily found. Did not the sacred texts say that he who sedulously practises Hatha Yoga acquired secret powers? They did: they were very practical and what could be more tempting to a busy man than the ability of being in two places at once? And there were the mysterious doctrines of Tantrism. Perhaps it would be wiser to hint at them, rather than bring them out into the full light of day. But surely it would be beguiling to suggest that those old sages knew ways of doubling and trebling the sexual powers? How it would astonish the little woman!

Thus began the age of the charlatans. The swamis themselves claimed to have these miraculous powers and they found Americans ready to believe them. America itself was something of a miracle. Amazing progress lay on every side. People were freely predicting that very soon man would discover the secret of flying through the air. Was it so impossible that these Indians, with their fathomless brown eyes and their mysterious chants, had discovered it long ago? The swamis said they had. True, they still collected their steamship fares from the faithful, but all that would be explained in the fullness of time, after one had done sufficient breathing up one nostril and down the other.

The swamis were so clever at explaining. There was the one who told, and even printed the story in his autobiography, of how, being late for a train, he and his companions had seen it moving out of the station. Exerting his secret powers, he brought it to a halt. How well he had dealt with the doubting Thomases who had said that perhaps the train had stopped because the signal had changed! He had replied, with a benevolent smile, that of course the signal had changed – that was all part of the miracle.

In India things went little better for the teachings of the Upanishads. There was no successor to Vivekananda. The Ramakrishna Mission went about their work, doing good as their master had wanted. Healing the sick and digging latrines are praiseworthy occupations. But the Indians were so very poor and there were so very many of them, that little time was left for meditation. As for the better classes, a profound torpor had settled upon them. There is a play by George Bernard Shaw called *The Tragedy of An Elderly Gentleman*, in which the gentleman in question finds himself among people who live two hundred years. They are such shining, self-assured beings that he dies, as he says, from sheer discouragement. The Indians felt that way. The English seemed to them so infinitely better in all their ways that there was nothing to do but to copy them. The upper classes sent their sons to the very schools which were set up to train their masters. They dressed in an English fashion, furnished their houses in an English style and read English books. Lawyers were proud to plead their cases in their torrid Courts of Law, dressed in frock-coats, striped trousers, a gown and a wig. The English despised Indian culture, and so, inevitably, did these Indians. The Upanishads went unread, even in the Indian universities. It was left to a German, Max Müller, to translate them. Indian mysticism became an embarrass-

Annie Besant, the prominent Theosophist and early propagandist for Indian freedom.

ment. Thomas Babington Macaulay, sent out to India to recommend an educational system, had dismissed the whole of Sanskrit literature, sacred or lay, as preposterous rubbish. He advised an English-style education, in English, and it was done as he wished. India still suffers from that monstrous piece of national vanity.

In such circumstances it is to be expected that it would be an English person who would make Indians conscious of their inheritance. Mrs Annie Besant had fallen in love with India. She was a vigorous, active woman who shared two of Vivekananda's characteristics. She had a magnificent platform presence, and she found Indians exasperating. She was quite unable to understand why they could not make an effort to govern themselves. There were the beginnings of a nationalist movement, but it devoted most of its time to sending messages of its undying loyalty to the British Crown.

To counter this supineness, she set up a school-cum-university where Indians could be Indians and proud of it. She campaigned for greater freedom for the country so vigorously that she was elected to the presidency of the Indian National Congress. She became a great figure in the land but a greater was waiting in the wings, Mahatma Gandhi. Besant found him if anything too Indian. She could make neither head nor tail of such theories as non-violence. She quarrelled with him, lost the battle, and faded into obscurity.

Her political rise and fall does not concern us here. Her interest lies in the fact that, almost unwittingly, she revived Indian mysticism. It was done in a roundabout way.

Annie Besant was a Theosophist. This was a brand-new religion which owed its existence to a Russian called Madame Blavatsky. (The 'Madame' seems obligatory among the now dwindling followers.) Like the swamis, she claimed mystic powers. She taught that all religions aimed at the same thing – to discover the Secret of the Universe. She said she knew it. Beyond the universe that we know is an 'astral' plane, a sort of spiritual fourth dimension. An initiate could inhabit this place. The secret of getting there had always been known, but only to a few, among whom she included, a little mysteriously, the Knights Templar, who lived so definitely in this world of the flesh, that they were disbanded by the Catholic Church for the practice of sodomy. She attracted a deal of attention from the upper classes of Europe and England by maintaining that spiritually-minded persons exuded a glow which she called an aura. She could tell from the colour of this aura the spiritual state of the owner. This doctrine she may have got from Tantrism: there was a great deal of the mysticism of the Upanishads in Theosophy, which was balanced by a very Western stress on helping humanity by good

Madame Blavatsky, the founder of the Theosophical movement.

works. Theosophy, complicated as it was, and defiantly esoteric, attracted a number of people with sharp intellects, perhaps because of those two characteristics. To Madame Blavatsky goes the credit of opening Western minds to Indian thought, in general, of which, till her, it was virtually ignorant.

Annie Besant did Trojan work in India to spread Theosophy, holding meetings all over India. A thirteen-year-old Indian boy from a well-bred family was taken to several such meetings by his English tutor. Looking back later in life, he recorded the experience:

There were metaphysical arguments, and discussions about reincarnation and the astral and other supernatural bodies, and auras, and the doctrine of Karma, and references not only to big books by Madame Blavatsky and other Theosophists but to the Hindu scriptures, the Buddhist 'Dhammapada', Pythagoras, Apollonius of Tyana, and various philosophers and mystics. I did not understand much that was said but it all sounded very mysterious and fascinating and I felt that here was the key to the secrets of the Universe. For the first time I began to think, consciously and deliberately, of religion and other worlds. The Hindu religion especially went up in my estimation; not the ritual or ceremonial part, but its great books, the 'Upanishads' and the 'Bhagavad Gita'. I did not understand them, of course, but they seemed very wonderful. I dreamt of astral bodies and imagined myself flying vast distances. This dream of flying high up in the air (without any appliance) has indeed been a frequent one throughout my life; and sometimes it has been vivid and realistic and the countryside seemed to lie underneath me in a vast panorama. I do not know how the modern interpreters of dreams, Freud and others, would interpret this dream.

So I became a member of the Theosophical Society at thirteen and Mrs Besant herself performed the ceremony of initiation, which consisted of good advice and instruction in some mysterious signs, probably a relic of freemasonry. I was thrilled. I attended the Theosophical Convention at Benares and saw old Colonel Olcott [a leading Theosophist] with his fine beard.

It is difficult to realise what one looked like or felt like in one's boyhood, thirty years ago. But I have a fairly strong impression that during these Theosophical days of mine I developed the flat and insipid look which sometimes denotes piety and which is (or was) often to be seen among Theosophist men and women. I was smug, with a feeling of being one-of-the-elect, and altogether I must have been a thoroughly undesirable and unpleasant companion for any boy or girl of my age.

Soon after [my tutor] F. T. Brooks left me I lost touch with Theosophy, and in a remarkably short time (partly because I went to school, in England) Theosophy left my life completely. But I have no doubt that those years with F. T. Brooks left a deep impress upon me and I feel that I owe a debt to him and to Theosophy. But I am afraid that Theosophists have since then gone down in my estimation. Instead of the chosen ones they seem to be very ordinary folk, liking security better than risk, a soft job more than the martyr's lot. But, for Mrs Besant, I always had the warmest admiration.

The boy was Jawaharlal Nehru, later to become Prime Minister of India. It is significant of the state into which Hinduism had fallen that so Indian a boy should have first heard of the Upanishads from what was virtually a foreign mission.

Annie Besant had a gifted eye for converts. Besides Theosophy, she was keen on the Boy Scouts. It was a new institution and she thought it would do Young

India a world of good. She selected a young convert in his twenties to drum up troops. He was lean, with piercing eyes, and an aggressively handsome face. She set him to organize Scout troops and he flung himself into the job with enthusiasm. He wore his shirt and shorts in a haphazard way, but he was a stickler for discipline. Any boy who was late (and this was almost a national characteristic) was sure to suffer from the scoutmaster's acid tongue. The sight of his son in this improbable uniform upset his father, but worse than short trousers was in store. The boy next turned up in a flowing robe gathered in at the waist by a blue cord. The scoutmaster has been transformed into another of Besant's ideas – Brothers of Service. He performed prodigies in this band, greatly impressing Mrs Besant, who felt that here she had the man on whose shoulders her Theosophical mantle would fall.

She took the young man to England where he was displayed as her star disciple. But the young man, like Nehru, had other fish to fry. His name was V. K. Krishna Menon. He parted with Theosophy and Besant. After prolonged vicissitudes, he rose to become an ambassador. The American public heard his denunciations of their policies from the tribune of the United Nations, and felt, in front of their televisions, much like the scout who was late.

Besant had still a third disciple whom her discerning eye picked out as a remarkable young man. Menon fell from power: J. Krishnamurti is still with us (1973) and is world-famous. It is he who revived the teaching of the Upanishads, and proclaimed them undefiled – at last.

Krishnamurti

He, too, was a handsome lad, but in a subtly beautiful way. He too, was taken to England and in due course deserted Annie Besant, who, poor lady, never did find her Theosophical Messiah.

To people who visualize a swami as all beard and beads sitting in an ashram, Krishnamurti is a surprise. He is clean-shaven, and in his old age perhaps even more handsome than he was when a boy. He does not dress the part at all, wearing what clothes are suitable to the country he is in. He does not live in an ashram. He has chosen Rome as his residence. He lives in the old quarter of the city, Trastevere, among Romans who for centuries have prided themselves on their indifference to religion, in spite of the Vatican being next door. He does not even claim to be a swami, although he is the most famous of them all.

I met him first in Bloomsbury when he was a young man and so was I. We nicknamed him The Messiah, but he made no show of being one. He sat in at our studio gatherings, listening to our ineffectual chatter. With youthful cruelty, we tried to draw him out, so that we could make fun of him. We asked for guidance, for spiritual uplift, or how to levitate. He listened and smiled. We grew to like him. We felt he was, or would be, a personality, like a young, roaring Welshman who occasionally flashed among us, Dylan Thomas.

When he broke away from Theosophy and began to gather his own disciples, we lost sight of him, and interest. I heard the story that he had addressed, in his perfect English, a meeting with persons from several countries, some of whom had no knowledge of the language in which he was speaking, yet everyone understood it. I dismissed it as claptrap. But later I was told that he had attacked the people who had started the rumour as a pack of hysterical women. He was not there to work miracles. What was he there to do? Nothing. That was the essence of his teaching.

Krishnamurti does not need me to put his doctrine into other words. His own are clear, precise and forceful. From here on I shall rely on them. He speaks a soft-voiced English, with occasional echoes of our Bloomsbury way of speaking, our flat a's, and our habit of shifting the accent back as far as we could on certain words. His tone is not emotional: it is at times offhand. He stops often to ask, 'Do you follow me?', with more than a hint that he is pretty sure his audience doesn't. Sometimes he says, '*Please* go on listening,' although his audience is spellbound. His style is the very reverse of that of his mentor, Annie Besant: she bellowed when her audience got the fidgets.

'It is important to understand from the very beginning,' he says, 'that I am not formulating any philosophy or any theological structure of ideas or theological concepts. It seems to me that all ideologies are idiotic. . . . If I were foolish enough to give you a system, and you were foolish enough to follow it, you would merely be copying, imitating, conforming, accepting. . . . If you try to study yourself according to another you will always remain a secondhand human being . . . because if we learn about ourselves according to someone else, we learn about *them*, not ourselves.'

The reader may remember the flower. According to the Upanishads, we must learn to look at it without calling it beautiful, because that is a word from the past that we have been taught. Krishnamurti applies this to our search for our true selves. No guru can really help us. He is something other, something outside us. How then are we to do it?

'Forget all you know about yourself: forget all you have ever thought about yourself: we are going to start as though we know nothing. It rained last night heavily, and now the skies are beginning to clear; it is a fresh day. Let us meet that fresh day as if it were the only day. Let us start on our journey together with all the remembrance of yesterday left behind – and begin to understand ourselves for the first time.'

He begins this new day for us on lines which, as we saw when we took that woman to the Caribbean, are the purest Upanishads.

'For centuries', he tells us, 'we have been conditioned by nationality, caste, class, tradition, language, education, literature, art, custom, convention, propaganda of all kinds, economic pressure, the food we eat, the climate we live in, our family, our friends, our experiences.'

The flow of items is impressive. It catches in its net almost everybody from Mowgli to Queen Elizabeth II (to take two extreme examples of environmental pressure). How are we to escape? Krishnamurti's answer goes beyond the Upanishads, and it is interesting to see why he does so. We are not required to examine our lives like peeling an onion. He shies away from this. He is afraid that if we brood too much on what has happened to us, we shall get too attached to our own autobiography. We shall be like those authors who assure us that they have forgotten all about their last book, then talk about it for the next hour. Krishnamurti wants us to throw away our past like an old boot.

But old boots are notoriously difficult to get rid of, as anybody who has gone fishing will know. Can we really take a completely indifferent attitude towards our influences, regarding them with a neutral eye, without long and painstaking study of the facts? Indeed, Krishnamurti is right; this may lead us astray; we may slip off that 'razor's edge' which the sages warned us about. Perhaps this is a risk we must take.

At this point an observation about Krishnamurti's personal life is due. The Irish have a saying about a priest who has been made a bishop: 'Now he'll never miss a meal and never hear the truth.' Krishnamurti was well on the way to being made a sort of bishop at an age when most of us were thinking about boys and girls. Theosophists and seekers after Oriental wisdom do not confess their sins. Krishnamurti has spent his life among these. Among all the current swamis and gurus, his is the most innocent face of all. I think he suffers a little from the same drawback as the Salvation Army. It lays so much stress on the single vice of alcohol because a glance at the lads and lassies shows that they know few others.

When he touches on intimate matters the results are not happy. He tells us all about ourselves like a schoolteacher briskly getting through an obligatory lesson in sex, hoping to end before the giggles start.

'Pleasure,' he admonishes us, 'is the structure of society. From childhood until death we are secretly, cunningly or obviously pursuing pleasure. So whatever our form of pleasure is, I think we should be very clear about it because it is going to guide and shape our lives.'

I am sure that is what we look like, the greedy mob of us, from the height of a lecture platform. But we don't pursue pleasure with all that eager heat. We do not rush straight from the lecture-hall to a five-course dinner and a night with houris. We may give that appearance as we crowd the exits. In truth, we go home, often enough, to dullness, boredom, and mindless television. Krishnamurti warns us against the pursuit of pleasure because, he says, if we don't get it, we will get pain. And since we secretly, cunningly, and so forth are *always* pursuing pleasure like satyrs after nymphs, it follows that all but the fleetest of hoof among the satyrs is in for a lot of unpleasantness.

Things are no better, it seems, for the satyr who catches his nymph. One nymph down, we up and want another, or so Krishnamurti says. 'It is the struggle to repeat and perpetuate pleasure which turns it into pain. Watch it in yourself.' Well, I've watched it, from childhood to maturity, and I cannot say I find it so. From the delights of gorging stolen apples as a boy to less bucolic pleasures of my later years, I do not find I have craved an immediate repetition. I once read a piece by the distinguished music critic Ernest Newman in which he said that, after a lifetime, he simply could not stand hearing Beethoven's symphonies any more. I agreed with him, and he and I gave up going to such concerts simultaneously. I do not think Krishnamurti gives sufficient weight to satiety. I hope, in his long and busy life, he has had an opportunity to experience it.

This antagonism to pleasure must bear a little further examination, for we shall find it in most of the modern mystics. It is not, be it marked, in the Upanishads. The sages specifically said that, having attained enlightenment about the real self, the enquirer could go back to chariots and women. They would appear to be illusions, compared to the Absolute, but there would be no great harm in driving around with one illusion seated in another. Yet by and large the Indian commentators, ancient and contemporary, gloss over this point. The explanation is that the Indian is, with few exceptions, a self-indulgent person, and he admits it. The consequence is that his pastors and masters are always trying to rein him in. The first act of the politicians, when India became free, was to ram home to each and every citizen that he was *not*. He was not free to drink alcohol, and to make that abundantly clear Prohibition was written into the Constitution. Kissing is not allowed on the Indian cinema screen, the official reason being that there are fears about the effect it will have on audiences.

The average Indian thinks of his own pleasures first, and then of his wife and family. He does not think much beyond that unless some great personality like Mahatma Gandhi forces him to. It has been the despair of the statesmen who, for a decade, have been trying to run the country on the ideas of Fabian Socialists, such as Bernard Shaw and Beatrice Webb. Indians break their hearts.

But I for one would not fault the Indian for his self-indulgence. He has the awesome authority of the Upanishads for it. Now there is one pleasure that we do tend to repeat, and that is eating. Exactly as Krishnamurti says, when we have enjoyed a good meal, four hours later or even less we yearn for another; and if we do not get it, undeniably there is pain. How are we to escape this dreadful dilemma? The Upanishadic sages come manfully to our aid.

The eighth section of the Tattiriya Upanishad says: 'Do not despise food. That shall be the rule. He who knows that food is established in food, becomes established. He becomes an eater of food, possessing food. He becomes great in offspring and cattle, and in the splendour of sacred wisdom, great in fame.'

The ninth section of the Tattiriya Upanishad is even more emphatic:

'Make for oneself much food. That shall be the rule. The earth, verily, is food: ether is the eater of food. In the earth is ether established, in ether is the earth established. Thus food is established in food. He who knows that food is established in food, becomes established. He becomes an eater of food, possessing food. He becomes great in offspring and cattle and in the splendour of sacred wisdom, great in fame.'

Whatever this may lack in strict Aristotelian logic is made up for in enthusiasm. This is brought out clearly in the mystical chant supplied at the conclusion of the Upanishad for the use of students and disciples.

'I am food, I am food, I am food. I am the food-eater. I am the food-eater. I am the food-eater. I am the first-born of the world order, earlier than the gods, on the centre of immortality. Such is the secret doctrine.'

For gourmets who may be attracted by these verses, I give a line or two of the original Sanskrit, which sounds very striking: the mantra, chanted at the beginning of it, is guaranteed to leave any headwaiter spellbound:

'aham annam, aham annam, aham annam; aham annadah, aham annadah, aham annadah'*

Krishnamurti is more on his home-ground when he leaves our greedy pursuit of pleasure to deal with other grounds of our unhappiness. The principal one of these is fear, and on this he has much to say that strikes home. A mind, he tells us, that lives in fear cannot move away from its own patterns of thinking, and this breeds hypocrisy. 'Living in such a corrupt, stupid society as we do, with the competitive education we receive, which engenders fear, we are all burdened with fear of some kind, and fear is a dreadful thing which warps, twists and dulls our days.'

Can we escape from it? The society that the Buddha and the sages turned their backs on was run by fear: fear of the gods unless they were propitiated; fear of misfortune should the right mantra not be said; fear of those darker things which the Tantrics dealt with. Krishnamurti, in telling us how to conquer fear, expounds the Upanishads with a brilliance and clarity which, in my opinion, betters all the other commentators, including the great Sankara.

Fear comes from thought – at least the social fears that he is dealing with. We project our experiences of the past, our knowledge of the disasters of others, and we are afraid of what may be in store for us. But, Krishnamurti reminds us, if

*Quoted from S. Radhakrishnan's standard text and translation, *The Principal Upanishads*, London 1953.

we are following his argument, then we have agreed to abandon thought, or, as I have put it previously, we must not call a rose beautiful, because that is an idea put into our heads by others.

You must withdraw yourself from fear. You must observe your fear without trying to judge it. There it is. Do not regard it as *your* fear, hall-marked with your personal initials. Do not criticize yourself at all, and particularly, do not search to fight it down with *courage*. Courage is another thing you have been taught.

I think I should interpolate something at this point. To ask that you should abandon courage is a difficult saying of Krishnamurti's. We most of us take courage as a virtue which we hope we have. But a young English writer that I knew found himself fighting the war against the Germans in Italy. He was a bookish man. To the astonishment of all his friends, he won the Military Cross for valour. In an act of great courage he, single-handed, wiped out a nest of machine-gunners. When I asked him why and how he had done it, he gave me a memorable answer: 'I was so desperately afraid of being thought a coward by the others.' I have quoted this to brave soldiers of many races, and they all agree that this is the truth.

To return to Krishnamurti. You are now observing fear, not as your fear, and not as something on which you can take action. You do not analyse it. You observe it as a whole.

His next and last step is one of great importance. You dismiss even the observer and find *you are* fear. When you see this, 'when you see that you are a part of fear, not separate from it, then,' says Krishnamurti, 'fear comes totally to an end.'

If that statement seems too sweeping, it should be remembered that Krishnamurti is not a psychologist, and not even an amateur one. It should be read in the general context of his thought. He is not concerned with unravelling our subconscious minds, still less the unconscious, a term which he looks upon with a jaundiced eye as probably having no real meaning. He is concerned with society – the pressures it puts on us, and the way to resist them. If we look at that society with detachment then we shall look at our fears about it with equal calm. We shall *note* what it can do, and has done to us. Throughout all his extensive lectures, Krishnamurti stresses that the real cause of our fears is our desire to please that society: in his favourite word of contempt, to be 'respectable'.

His originality is plain when he discusses freedom. It will be remembered that it was John Stuart Mill's writings on this subject that so moved Vivekananda and led, in part, to that bronze statue in Bombay. It would be interesting to hear a discussion of freedom between Mill and Krishnamurti. Mill, I think, would have been scandalized: he was the epitome of the respectable man.

Freedom, says Krishnamurti, is not freedom *from* something. It is a state of mind. Krishnamurti relies on his belief, rather than on logic, in this matter but it can be argued quite elegantly: The laws of England guarantee my freedom, but no law can guarantee my freedom from the law.

What then, is this 'state of mind'? It is, says Krishnamurti, 'freedom to doubt and question everything and therefore so intensive and active and vigorous that it throws away every form of dependence, slavery, conformity and acceptance.' It is a state, he says, in which there is no leadership, no tradition and no authority.

It is a doctrine which should appeal to the young: but Krishnamurti adds a rider that may not. To be in this state of mind you must be alone: not the aloneness of fifteen minutes' meditation with the door locked, but something much more drastic:

'To be alone you must die to the past. When you are alone, totally alone, not belonging to any family, any nation, any culture, any particular continent, there is that sense of being an outsider.'

We can imagine how that would have set John Stuart Mill arguing, and sent Vivekananda into a rage. The same things happen when people hear Krishnamurti say it today. To all of that he has a simple answer: that state of freedom cannot be argued about. It is beyond consciousness.

We have seen that when Ramakrishna spoke about the love of God, he was vague about what he meant. Krishnamurti is brutally clear:

'When you say you love God what does it mean? It means that you love a projection of your own imagination, a projection of yourself clothed in certain forms of respectability, according to what you think is noble and holy: so to say, "I love God", is absolute nonsense. When you worship God you are worshipping yourself.'

By this he does not mean that real self: he means that excellent person that you try to persuade your children that you are. So Krishnamurti has demolished one term of the statement, 'I love God.' God has gone. But Krishnamurti does not demolish love. He is fascinated by it. He elevates it above all other things. But it is his own peculiar form of love. No ardent female disciple should take it as an invitation to love Krishnamurti, nor as giving a hope that he will love her. Krishnamurti's love can only be described in his own eloquent words:

'Fear is not love, jealousy is not love, dependence is not love, possessiveness and domination is not love, responsibility and duty is not love, self-pity is not love, the agony of not being loved is not love, love is not the opposite of hate any more than humility is the opposite of vanity. So if you can eliminate all these, not by forcing them but by washing them away as the rain washes the dust of many days from a leaf, then perhaps you will come upon this strange flower which man always hungers after.'

I admire the prose; I do not know exactly what it means, but I am sure it could not be better said. In all the Hindu mystics, however clear their words or simple their parables, there is always something at the heart of their teaching which escapes words. 'Do it yourself', they say, 'and see.'

It is the same with Krishnamurti. It remains that he is by far the best exponent of the Upanishads living today, and he will long be remembered by those who take the trouble to read him. But I do not think that such a total rebel will ever have a statue put up for him.

Krishnamurti with Mrs Besant, 1926. Photo Radio Times Hulton Picture Library.

Bhaktivedanta Swami Prabhupada, founder of the Krishna Consciousness movement (Hare Krishna).

Krishna Consciousness

We shall need all we have gathered of the history of Hindu mysticism to treat the next swami fairly. Seen in the light of that, he is understandable: seen in the light of the little coloured electric lights with which he likes to surround himself, he is distinctly less appealing.

The Krishna Consciousness movement is a mid-twentieth century phenomenon. Its dancing disciples burst upon the world like the hippies, with whom they are often confused, but whom, in fact, they zealously loathe. They have 63 branches in 12 countries. How many members they have is more doubtful. Other Hindu mystics have told me that it is fewer than usually supposed: they make so much noise wherever they are that people think there must be a lot of them: but that, of course, may be no more than a little backbiting among the swamis.

The dancing disciples are liable to pop disconcertingly around corners on the Lower East Side, in Bloomsbury Square or the Boul' Mich', but they and their cult are best studied in the land of their origin, India. It is true that there the orthodox Hindu often enquires, 'Who are these jackanapes?', to which His Divine Grace A. C. Bhaktivedanta Swami Prabhupada is wont to reply, 'Who are these fools and rascals who know nothing of their own religion?' His Divine Grace is quite right: for all their apparent eccentricities, the followers of Krishna Consciousness are deeply rooted in India's past.

Swami Prabhupada's headquarters are in Bombay, a bustling, commercial city of six million people, dotted with skyscrapers, and which contains more sceptical agnostics per acre than any other place in India. Occasionally His Divine Grace conducts a slap-up revivalist mission to convert them. Even for the most blasé traveller, it is a sight not to be missed.

A huge tent is erected downtown, capable of holding ten thousand people. The tent is liberally illuminated by coloured lights in naked bulbs. Powerful loudspeakers blare from every angle, outside and in. The proceedings begin at six in the morning and continue until late in the evening, to the vast annoyance of surrounding residents. Entrance is free. As the loudspeakers say, in the dulcet rumble of Ivy League accents, 'Come inside: we have provided you with chairs to sit on, mattresses to squat on. Come in and listen to our fine, decent boys singing kirtans, see the worship of our Lord Krishna, then at 7.30 p.m. precisely, listen to the words of the Living Reincarnation of the Lord, His Divine Grace Bhaktivedanta Swami Prabhupada.' A large poster informs us that His Divine Grace is five hundred years old.

The voice comes from a young man on a platform outside the main entrance. It is midday, when Bombayites have a brief respite from the air-conditioned hustle of the skyscrapers. He has gathered quite a crowd.

'Don't listen to me,' he implores us. 'I feel quite ashamed when people prefer to stay here and not go inside to see the Lord Krishna. I am just his humble disciple.' We do not budge: we are enjoying this transparent piece of self-promotion. The young man is American and it is to be expected. He bears a marked resemblance to Gore Vidal. He has Mr Vidal's watchful but slightly abstracted gaze which he assumes when he has just thought of something brilliant to say and is waiting for the moment to pounce. He even sits in a baroque arm-chair, similar to that which Mr Vidal uses in his beautiful Rome apartment, only much less expensive. Behind him is a sunburst of fairy-lamps, meant to enhalo the young man's head, but which unfortunately has come off one hook and is lopsided. To his right is a ten-foot long banner saying QUESTIONS, to his left one equally long, saying ANSWERS. The young man has a shaven head, a top-knot, a saffron robe and elegant rimless spectacles.

'Well, come on then', he pleads. 'Ask questions. That's what I am here for. What are you afraid of?'

A business man of fifty clears his throat.

'I am afraid of death.'

Indians delight in debate, but their procedure is inclined to be elliptical. The disciple is taken off balance for a moment. Then the Gore Vidal look comes back into his eye.

'There is no death,' he says. 'If you believe in the Lord Krishna there is no death. Look.' He seizes his robe. 'This is the only possession I have in the world.' We are suitably impressed; the copy of the Bhagavad Gita he has on his knee, and his spectacles, he presumably borrowed from His Divine Grace. He continues. 'I shall change this robe after ten years. When I put on a new one, I won't change. Your body is like this robe. Death is just putting on a new one.'

An American devotee of Krishna Consciousness on the Question and Answer throne.

A youth puts up his hand.

'What would I have to do if I joined Krishna Consciousness?' he asks. By his aquiline nose and pale complexion I judge him to be a Parsee. They are inveterate joiners.

The disciple ticks the items off on his fingers. 'You would have to worship the Lord Krishna by chanting the holy mantra, "Hare Krishna, Hare Krishna, Hare Rama Hare Rama Hare Hare Hare!" You would have to eat only vegetables. You would have to be chaste, but you may have a wife, but only one. You would have to obey His Divine Grace.'

The Parsee looks a little distressed.

'Why should I have to be a vegetarian?'

'For the purity of your body,' says the disciple. 'I am not an Indian. I am just a coarse American. But I revere the ancient wisdoms of your country. Read the Vedas,' he says, when a voice from the crowd says, none too politely:

'Do you?'

We turn to look. The questioner is tall, youngish, and dressed in the latest mod fashion from London, with a wide tie, luxuriant sideburns, and a moustache.

'I beg your pardon,' says the disciple, twisting the robe that must last ten years, a little haughtily across him.

'I said, "Do *you* read the Vedas?"'

'Of course I do.'

'I doubt it. Because if you did you will find that at the time of the Vedas the Hindus ate meat.'

There are some surprised murmurs in the crowd and then some one begins a hooting little chuckle, 'Hoo-hoo. Hoo-hoo.'

It is a Hindu dressed in national dress. He has the stoop and look of a professor.

'Hoo-hoo. Hoo-hoo,' he says. 'Quite right. Absolutely right,' and he begins to quote Sanskrit. The disciple looks miserable, but by a mercy the professor makes his way out of the crowd saying, 'Hoo-hoo, hoo-hoo, these foreigners, these foreigners. Hoo-hoo.'

There is an embarrassed silence. We look encouragingly at the disciple but he is still miserable.

'All right,' he mutters sadly, watching the professor retreat. 'Go away if you want to.' Then in a little-boy voice, caught by the microphone, 'I don't mind.'

I think it will be helpful to say something. I say: 'May I ask a question?' The sound of English spoken without an Indian accent seems to encourage the disciple.

'Of course you may, sir. What is it?'

'In that copy of the Gita you have on your lap,' I say, and he nods cheerfully, 'you will find that Krishna encourages Arjuna to kill his relatives. Would *you* kill *your* relatives?'

The Gore Vidal look returns to his eyes. A smile spreads slowly across his lips.

'Willingly,' he says.

A shout of laughter goes up from the crowd. India's worst plague is relatives. The disciple blushes, composes his face and adds demurely, 'If the Lord Krishna told me to.'

'Well answered,' says the man who feared death, shooting a triumphant glance at me, for the disciple has clearly won him over.

The disciple sees his moment.

'But why ask me these questions? Why not go inside and ask His Divine Grace. Why stand in the hot sun? We have chairs for you to sit on, mattresses for you to squat on. See our fine boys singing our kirtans. I am just a humble disciple . . .'

The shrine of Krishna in the Krishna Consciousness ashram. Meditation follows worship, after which the doors of the shrine are closed.

Inside the great tent are, indeed, the chairs and mattresses, and a large number of people moving around. Large pictures of Krishna decorate the canvas walls showing him stealing the curds, sporting with the cow-girls and, grown-up, driving Arjuna's chariot. The style is that of pictures of the Virgin or the Sacred Heart of Jesus which are hung up in Italian bedrooms. Posters tell us what we must do to be saved, and it is very much what the American told us outside. We must be devoted to Krishna.

The young god himself is at the far end of the tent, a rather effeminate looking boy, blue, in the shape of a statue, or, as the modern Hindu is learning to call it, with a stiff upper-lip, an idol. He is on an altar, surrounded by lights and a profusion of flowers. An elderly woman fans him with a fan of peacock feathers. Beside him is another statue, this time of a woman. This is Radha, his I-Don't-Know-What-To-Call-Her-Without-Offending-Somebody. At all events, she was the wife of a local farmer. She fell in love with Krishna and he with her. Theirs was a happy, playful love. With a sociability rare in young lovers, Krishna and Radha invite everybody to share their happiness in each other. This may be attained in two ways. One is by offering them tasty things to eat. Someone is

Close-up of the Krishna Consciousness shrine. A devotee fans the statues of Krishna and his consort Radha.

doing that now, setting down a silver dish in front of the statues. The lovers do not eat the food: the worshipper does that. But as he eats, the gift of gaiety and happiness is passed on to him or her.

Seated on the chairs (as advertised) are about a thousand men and women, following the rite. They look glum, but that is probably because the chairs are exceeding hard. People on the mattresses look happier. Joy, however, is unconfined on a small platform to the right of the altar. Here young men in saffron robes are worshipping Krishna in the second of the two ways that Krishna likes: they are beating drums, dancing, and singing. Dancing as worship has occurred throughout history and in many climes. David, it will be recalled, danced naked in front of the Ark of the Lord. As a boy, being interested both in religion and the ballet, I would sometimes try to imagine David's choreography, but he obstinately turned out to be an Isadora Duncan without the swathes. Krishna Consciousness have got rid of this difficulty. Their dancing is of a most elementary character, consisting of hopping from one foot to the other. This obviously gives pleasure to the dancer, and wild delight to the street urchins of India's cities, for when they see a foreign hippy, they caper round him in a light-footed version of the Krishna stomp.

The Kirtan *group by the shrine and in front of the ashram.*

(Overleaf) The world famous Hare Krishna hop.

The drummer at the Krishna Consciousness session in Bombay.

From time to time the drummer who accompanies this ritual increases the pace of his rhythm in a frenzied break. The dancers increase the rate of their hopping, but not quite as much, this being too much to ask from simple devotees, who, as the man outside has told us, are unpaid. Amid heavy breathing the dance comes to an end. At the altar, a woman waves a tray of burning oil lamps in front of the two statues. This routine goes on all day until the evening when His Divine Grace A. C. Bhaktivedanta Swami Prabhupada takes his seat on a throne between the dancing platform and the altar.

Signboards at the entrance to the ashram of Chinmayananda and, below, to Hare Krishna Land. >

(Overleaf) The whole Kirtan group.

ISKCON

ॐ

Founder Acarya

His Divine Grace A.C. BHAKTIVEDANTA Swami Prabhupāda

HARE KRISHNA LAND

For a man five hundred years old he looks very fit. For a man in his seventies who has had a serious illness, he looks much as one would expect. He has grandfatherly eyes, a broad flat nose, and a generous mouth. He has impressive ears, like those on the statues of the Buddha, out of which hair grows in abundance. He has close-cropped grey hair and he does not shave regularly every day. Disciples have explained to me that every one of his facial features that I have described are signs of his Divinity, though I assume that this would not include the stubble on his chin, this being too transient.

Some several thousand people are now in the tent. His Divine Grace sits silent while people kiss his feet. This is done to all swamis, the feet being held to exude a potent spiritual influence. An awed hush falls upon the assembly. Many of its members believe that he is the incarnation of God Himself, but they are misinformed. A more careful study of the literature of the movement reveals that he is the reincarnation of Chaitanya, who lived at the end of the fifteenth century.

Chaitanya was a saint who had, and has, innumerable followers, but they did not include Vivekananda who, in characteristic style, said that Chaitanya had turned his native province into a land of effeminate cowards and caused Bengal to lose its manliness. For once the orthodox Brahmins agreed with Vivekananda; from the very beginning they regarded Chaitanya as a thorough pest.

He was devoted to the point of infatuation to Krishna and Radha. He summed up his teaching thus:

'I crave only to repeat your name [Krishna's] so that my eyes shall ever overflow with tears, my mouth utter only broken syllables, my breath be suffocated with emotion, my soul filled with joy and my body covered with goosepimples.'

He was opposed to the Vedas and the teaching of Sankara. He wished all religion to be choc-a-bloc with emotion. He would lead his disciples, singing and dancing, through the streets. He taught that since Krishna loved cow-girls, the devotee should love Krishna like a girl, which gives substance to Vivekananda's complaint.

Today, groups of followers of Chaitanya will go round to private houses, if invited, to rouse this passion in the householder and his family. These men would scorn to be thought of as followers of His Divine Grace, for whom they have hard words. I attended one such gathering. A drummer and some men in saffron robes sang while sitting in a circle. An interminably long sermon followed. This was supposed to rouse the religious emotions of the listeners to fever pitch. Since it was delivered in a regional language, an interpreter was provided to whisper in my ear the fiery words. Having whispered ten leaden platitudes in my ear he

< *Close-up of the shrine to Kali on the wall of the*
Shahi-Hamdan mosque in Srinagar, shown on p. 125.

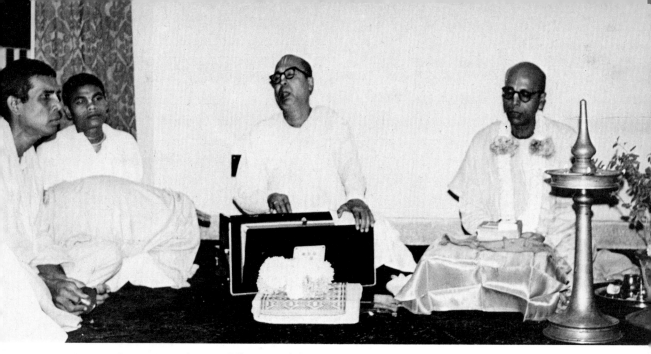

In a private house, followers of the mystic Chaitanya worship Krishna with ecstatic singing and chanting.

relapsed into silence, numbed, presumably, by the next ten. Nobody got goose-flesh. There was, however, one tense moment. The preacher stopped his sermon to complain that the head of the household was showing the soles of his feet. The head was a distinguished banker with the control of vast sums of money, but he obediently withdrew his offending extremities and tucked them under him. I do not know what was wrong with them, and I was too polite to ask: I can only say that, in my experience, bankers' feet do seem to lack spirituality.

To return to the tent. His Divine Grace speaks with a gravelly voice. In view of all that surrounds him, one is not, at first, inclined to take what he has to say with seriousness. But that is a mistake. Swami Prabhupada has done some important thinking. Starting out in life as a university professor of philosophy, he has seen a danger in Hindu mysticism, and his movement is designed to deal with it.

We have noted that there are many paths to the real self. Thus Hatha Yoga, the discipline of the body, is one of them. The highest is Raja Yoga, by which inner tranquillity is attained solely through thought and meditation. Prabhupada is a down-to-earth man and he saw that this latter path is well beyond the capacities of the majority of people. Such continuous use of the mind to achieve the cessation of all mental processes can probably be undertaken only by persons who have had an academic training in some discipline, such as philosophy, history, mathematics and such, whether in public or in private studies. He must, at least, have some knowledge of how to use his mental power in research. A person without this can often fall into despair; worse, he can deceive himself that he has attained some enlightenment, when he has not. Then, finding he has not attained tranquillity, he will feel utterly disappointed.

Prabhupada saw this problem. He set out to solve it. We can understand his solution better if we draw a Western parallel. From the earliest days of Christianity sex was a problem. The instincts of the Early Church were towards chastity, if only to contrast themselves with the pagans whose instincts were all against it. Converts rolled into the Church in great numbers, but many wondered, if God wanted them to be chaste, why had he made them lewd? St Augustine, Bishop of Hippo, set himself down at the desk to explain. It could have been done in a pamphlet. Augustine, being a prolific writer, composed a very long book, and Augustine being also a great literary genius, the book was a masterpiece. In the course of answering the problem Augustine ranged over the whole of known history, giving, almost incidentally, a dazzling picture of the fall of Rome. In the heart of all this was the theory of original sin, which explained that we inherited our lusts from our first parents, Adam and Eve. His book, *The City of God*, is read by all candidates for holy orders, because they have to, but nowadays, it is not read much by anybody else. St Augustine had solved the problem, but in a complicated way.

Robert Baden Powell faced the same problem when he came to found the Boy Scout movement. I do not know whether 'B.P.' had read *The City of God*, but he knew boys and was aware that they had their fair share of original sin. So he simply inserted a clause in the Boy Scout Law: 'A Scout is clean in thought, word and deed,' and that was that. Some boys were: many tried. The moral elevation of the movement was made clear, at all events.

Swami Prabhupada is the Baden Powell of the Indian mystics. He has devised a faith of childlike simplicity. The first steps along the path to self-realization are always difficult. Swami Prabhupada has turned them into a toddle. He is a follower of Chaitanya, and therefore holds the Bhagavad Gita in high esteem. The Gita, as we have seen, is a complicated book. Part of it is based squarely on the Upanishads: part of it is a glorification of the god Krishna. Prabhupada barely glances at the Upanishadic sections, though he acknowledges that they are there and does not dispute them. He concentrates on the worship of Krishna.

Even this he simplifies in a manner that makes it understandable to the young. All you have to do (but put your heart in it) is to repeat the mantra, 'Hare Krishna, Hare Krishna, Krishna Krishna Hare Hare, Hare Rama, Hare Rama, Rama Rama, Hare Hare.' If you pour out your love for Krishna in these simple words, he and Radha will pour out their love to you.

The appeal is obvious. Krishna and Radha are Mum and Dad, but miraculously never growing old. Radha loves Dad eternally: divorce will never raise its head in their household. Krishna is for ever gay and always ready for a romp: was he not famous for his high spirits when he was young? If you join this happy family you can dance, and clap your hands, and beat away at a drum making as much noise as you like. Mum and Dad like noise. Swami Prabhupada's way of treating his disciples as children is sometimes blatant. There are rules against taking drugs and alcohol, as might be expected. But there is also a rule against taking *tea* or *coffee*. What then are you to drink, besides water? Obviously – milk.

Krishna Consciousness has made little impression on India: it has even aroused antagonism. Prabhupada's insistence on Krishna as the True God is offensive to those who follow Vishnu and Siva. Hinduism is a religion quite without dogmas. It has no Pope. When the Chinese invaded Tibet, the Dalai Lama (who is both God and Pope) fled to India, the land from which his Buddhist faith came. He found his welcome less than warm. When Pope Paul VI came to Bombay he, personally, made a good impression. But I am still asked by Hindus how Catholics can allow one very human man to lay down the law as to what they should believe.

In the West, and particularly in the United States, things went much better for Swami Prabhupada. He began operations there in the early 'sixties, a time of vertiginous change in the manner and customs of all Western civilization. There had been some sort of a revolution earlier, but by now it had faded. Its flag-bearers, Jack Kerouac and Allen Ginsberg, had fallen into that self-assertive Whitmanesque clamouring which is the plague of American writing. The Dharma-bums had a tenuous connection with Indian thought (Dharma-bums could mean that they were fated to wander) inasmuch as they began by turning their backs on the established order. Allen Ginsberg did visit India. He dressed in a dhoti to express his attachment to Indian things. The dhoti is essentially a white garment, if possible, spotlessly white. Ginsberg preferred a parti-coloured one of his own design. He was immediately put down as just another American eager to teach Indians how things should be done. Having recited some verses judged to be obscene, he would have been turned out of the country had it not been for the good-humoured intervention of Nehru.

In the American mind, the idea of India was now associated with irresponsible behaviour mixed up with drugs. This proved distasteful to many of the younger generation who were seeking a way out from the catastrophes of broken families, a repressive way of life devoted to material things, and later a clumsy, cruel and stupid war.

An American attached to the Ramakrishna movement in Bombay (the 'Question–Answerer' reported in the text).

Prabhupada presented them with a way of life of an Arcadian simplicity. It is no wonder that he found followers. He opened his mission on the Lower East Side in New York in an empty shop, fitted with nothing but mats on the floor. One of his earliest disciples, with the swami's permission, has recorded an incident. Two or three were gathered together to listen to the swami, when an old, grey Bowery drunk entered. He carried a pack of paper hand-towels and a roll of toilet paper. He walked past the Swami, placed the towels and the toilet paper carefully on a sink, and left. Prabhupada rose to the occasion.

'Look,' he said, 'he has just begun his devotional service. Whatever we have – it doesn't matter what – we must offer to Krishna.'

American mothers and fathers write anxiously to the swami enquiring about their sons who have followed him. They fear that there are involvements in dubious and arcane doings. They need not fear. There are no hidden depths in Prabhupada. His simplicity has deep roots. He is teaching first steps, like the Latin master who tells us that if we get 'Balbus built a wall' correct, we will one day read Cicero.

Besides, there is another thing. Just after the Second World War, a great number of young American men went into monasteries. There was much talk of a great religious wave sweeping America. It did not sweep the Vatican. I remember a prelate there saying, 'Ah, well. They'll be out in two years.' They were.

The survival of Tantrism

The Bhagavad Gita, then, is still very much alive. So, unfortunately, is Tantrism. This, it will be remembered, taught that adepts at meditation and such could acquire supernatural powers: in a word, he or she could work miracles. Since this is a chapter about miracles, it is well to pause at its beginning and think a moment of Christiaan Barnard.

Barnard is an able surgeon who specializes in operations on the heart. The heart is nothing more than a muscle. The medical profession had known for some years that this muscle could be taken out of a person recently dead and transferred to a person whose heart had ceased to function. The transplanted muscle could be made to work, for how long and for what benefit to the patient was not known. Christiaan Barnard transplanted a heart, and the patient lived, at least for a while.

He lived long enough for a wave of hysteria to sweep the world. Barnard had performed a mechanical operation. It needed enormous skill and a team of assistants, but it was still mechanical. It could be performed by other men. But the public took the attitude that Barnard had raised a man from the dead, as Lazarus was raised by Jesus. The world yearned for a miracle, and made Barnard a miracle man. This was no fault of the surgeon. Curtis Bill Pepper, his official biographer, has been my friend for many years, and many are the discussions we have had about the subject. I am certain, from those and Pepper's detailed book, that Barnard at no time considered that he had done anything miraculous. At the most he considered himself a front-rank surgeon with, perhaps, an extra touch of daring. He accepted with good grace the criticisms of his professional peers, who doubted if he had added much to medical knowledge. Unluckily, he was handsome. He had the right looks for a worker of miracles, and, for a while, the miracle man he remained. When the dead he had raised failed to stay alive, the public turned its back on him. It had no use for a fine surgeon. It wanted marvels. Barnard, unable to supply them, slipped into obscurity.

India has always been, in a large proportion, an illiterate country. It has also been poor. If the literate West could yearn for miracles, it is no wonder that Indians do. Where there is yearning for the marvellous, there will be those ready to supply it. Nor are they necessarily deceivers. Imagine yourself for a moment laying your hand on the head of a child and finding that a fever has subsided, and imagine that you have done it in some poor peasant village, in Calabria, say, or Mexico. See in your mind's eye the press of awed villagers, the sick children held out to you, the halt, the lame and the blind who congregate outside your door each morning, begging for your touch. Think whether you would dismiss the whole thing with angry contempt, or whether you would say to yourself that perhaps, just perhaps, there were more things in heaven and earth than were dreamt of in your philosophy.

I do not believe in miracles at all. Here, in this brief chapter, are some people who do.

Mataji Nirmala Devi, the Divine Mother as she is called, is a handsome woman in her middle age, with a rather rounded face and motherly eyes. Her husband is a high civil servant. Both are rich in their own right. They live in a large, cool apartment in the best quarter of Bombay. She is not a Hindu: she was brought up as a Christian. She thinks that God is the same in any religion, and she should know because she does not deny that she is God herself. God's manners are those of a sophisticated and charming hostess.

The Divine Mother, Mataji Nirmala Devi, who is reputed to be capable of curing the sick.

She says she was aware that she had special powers even as a child, and that her parents thought so too. She was nurtured in a respectable Christian household. No crocodile seized her ankle, she did not go into trances, she had no desire to dress as a man. She went regularly to Mass and had no visions. Since she felt that she had power to heal, she studied to be a doctor in order to know what went on in the human body. She also studied the Tantric doctrine of the Kundalini, the coiled serpent that lies between the legs, and can be incited to rise in the body. She draws diagrams of it as she talks.

She cures by vibrations. She is generous about these. They are not her private property. We all have them. Ours are often negative. Hers are positive. If we wish to receive them, we hold out our hands to her. The Kundalini will do the rest.

Her devotees are people of the middle class to which she belongs, dressed, when women, in normal saris. They gaze at her with the happy half-smile of members of a women's club listening to a good-looking young poet. Her favourite disciple is a girl in her early twenties, who talks readily of her experience.

< A girl whom Nirmala Devi cured of hysterical attacks that contorted her body and face.

The man, described below, who was suffering from leukaemia and has become a devotee of Nirmala Devi.

As a child this disciple was a hysteric. Before she met Nirmala Devi, she often had seizures which constricted her hands so that they became like claws. She still talks in an excited fashion, with many of the gestures of an hysteric. But, disconcertingly, her conversation is sober and clear. Her expression is relaxed. Her tranquillity shines through her.

Another disciple is a man, also of the prosperous middle classes, who contracted cancer of the white blood cells – leukaemia. It is invariably fatal. He went to New York to attend a cancer centre there, as a last resort. They gave him little hope, but they were ready to do what they could. It would cost between twenty and fifty thousand dollars. Even if he had that amount of money to start with, Indian exchange restrictions would have prevented him from spending it. He returned to India, resigned to die. He met Nirmala Devi. In leukaemia the white cells proliferate enormously, and had been doing so without stop. Now his cell count went down. It is still doing so. It has given him an extra lease of life, but he has none of the usual wild optimism of a seriously sick man who sees his symptoms diminishing. 'I may die at any moment,' he says. 'But I am grateful to the Mother.'

She holds meditation classes which fill large halls. She gives simple talks on the Tantric doctrine of the Kundalini, mixed with a pinch of the Upanishads (the word from cooking recipes leaps to the mind: her tone and manner are so much those of the mistress of a well-run house). She gives wise warnings against other miracle-workers who promise powers for evil purposes. The audience holds out its hands to her to receive the vibrations.

She is not allowed, by law, to cure cancer in the United States, though she has disciples there.

Those are the facts, but there are not nearly enough of them. As a doctor trained in Western methods, it is strange that she has not had her cures checked in clinics. An ordinary observer can see she has done a world of good to the once hysterical girl. The doctor of the man with leukaemia confirms the fall in his cell-count, but ventures no opinion as to its cause, little being known about the disease. She does some good and no harm at all. Whether she really cures the sick can only be decided by a commission of doctors. She has never called one. Perhaps, in the course of her medical studies, she discovered that doctors have negative vibrations.

With Sai Baba we are on to more cheerful topics. He is a tall, happy man with a huge shock of hair which he wears in an Afro cut. He has a huge following which in this vast country can be counted in millions. They are far from being poor and illiterate. One of his most fervent believers is Harry Saltzman, the producer of the James Bond films.

Part of Satya Sai Baba's appeal is that he claims to be an incarnation of another Sai Baba (AD 1856–1916). This first Sai Baba has an even greater appeal than his reincarnation. His picture can be seen enshrined up and down the country. At great Hindu festivals his statues can be seen elevated to equal rank with those of the gods. I cannot explain this: I must let such facts as there are speak for themselves.

Sai Baba the Elder was not a Hindu at all. He was a Moslem. Islam does not admit mysticism. Such mystics as the Sufi are considered heretics and in the past have been put down with fire and sword. Sai Baba frequented, however, Indian temples, where he worked minor miracles, such as turning water into oil. One irate Moslem tried to kill him with a club, but Sai Baba caught his wrist in time. Thus preserved, Sai Baba convinced his followers that he had special powers. He could read people's minds: he could cure illnesses while hundreds of miles from the patients: he could predict the future. He was publicly worshipped by Hindus. He gave advice, but gave no mantras, or special rituals. He never spoke of Yoga, or the Kundalini. The ashes from his fire were considered to have a special potency for good.

Shrine of Sai Baba (see pages 62–3).

If I call these facts, I do not mean that they are historical facts. Sai Baba wrote nothing: his speech was reported by avowed disciples. The books and pamphlets about him are made up of word-of-mouth reports and are otherwise unsupported. His cult resembles that of Christiaan Barnard: it was founded on emotion and a yearning for the miraculous. Before he died, he predicted that he would return after death. To this day, Indian followers, when faced with a difficult decision, write out the alternatives on slips of paper, put them under Sai Baba's picture, and settle the question by drawing lots.

They can, of course, consult Sai Baba in the flesh: that is to say they can go to *Satya* Sai Baba. That is a much more dramatic affair. Sai Baba performs miracles as a routine. His favourite one is to wave his hand in the air and produce sacred ashes. He has been known to do this in the unlikely setting of the Rotary Club of Bombay. Another miracle has great charm. Authors all know the misery of being presented with a copy of their book and asked to write something in it on the spur of the moment. Most of us lock ourselves in the bathroom a while and try to think of something to say. Not so Sai Baba. It is *he* who presents the book to distinguished visitors. The visitor turns to the flyleaf hoping to find his name. It is blank. Smilingly, Sai Baba invites him to close the book, and makes conversation about other matters. Then he asks his visitor to open the book once more. Lo! on the title page is a dedication in the swami's own hand.

He has another Siddhi which has done nothing to diminish the number of his followers. He materializes gold rings out of thin air, and gives them away. A story about one of these rings is narrated in his official biography.

An American woman visited him, and he obliged her by materializing out of thin air the customary gold ring. It was set with red and green precious stones, in the traditional Indian fashion. The American woman was dumbfounded. She wore the ring for a while, but then discovered that she did not like it. She firmly believed in Sai Baba's miraculous powers, but she was not so sure of his taste in jewellery. She felt that she could not take the ring off, but every time she looked at it, she very much wanted to. She told her dilemma to her friends. Soon she met Sai Baba again. With a sweet smile, he waved his hand in the air, and produced another ring, this time of a thoroughly Western design.

There may be two opinions about Sai Baba's mystic powers, but there can be no doubt about his beautiful manners.

I think at this point I should introduce the 'Maharishi'. He does not produce gold rings, but he has worked an even greater miracle. He has persuaded the Pentagon to include a course of transcendental meditation in its training course. It was a bold

'Maharishi' at home, holding flowers which are symbols of love and peace.
Photo K. N. Ramanathan (Camera Press, London).

decision for the Pentagon: not only was the teaching exotic, it gave a handle to the Pentagon's critics who maintained they had been in a state of trance for years.

His real name is Maharshi Yogi, and he was a humble run-of-the-mill New York swami for many years, until he suddenly came to fame. The West corrupted his name into 'Maharishi'. This means 'great rishi' and rishis were sages who lived in remote places, undergoing severe austerities. Maharshi Yogi, I need not say, is not one of these. It is impossible to imagine a true rishi who giggles: and Maharshi Yogi would not be himself if he did not.

He gained notoriety when the Beatles, their exceptional talents fading, went to him for advice. They told him their troubles, which were multitudinous. Maharshi Yogi listened, and giggled. This was a new sound to these much flattered young men, though not the new sound they were desperately in need of. They left in a towering huff.

Yet of all the contemporary swamis, 'Maharishi' represents most clearly what the Upanishads are all about. It is well-known that he makes his journeys in a private aircraft. This is perfectly in accord with the texts. Not only can he use an aeroplane, he could even make love to the hostess if he wanted to, without offending the canon. The Upanishads explicitly state that a man, having meditated and found release, can return to the world and (as we have seen) 'enjoy chariots and women'. He will probably look upon both with amused detachment, and that is exactly how Maharshi Yogi looks upon the world.

Mataji Nirmala Devi, whose curative powers represent a survival of Tantrism. >

(Overleaf) Inside Chinmayananda's ashram in Bombay.

Rajneesh

Before I write about Bhagwan Shree Rajneesh I must, as they say in the British House of Commons, 'declare my interest'. That is to say, I must confess any personal matter which might prejudice my judgment.

Rajneesh began his career as a professor of philosophy, taking up that of a swami only after a deep study of comparative systems. In his ashram he has an enviable library of books. He advises his disciples which of these they should read, and to which passages they should pay attention. He marks these passages with scholarly neatness: one dot for a notable passage, two dots for those which are very notable. He has one of my books on his shelves. In it I describe my own experience of the Upanishads. I value the fact that I have several dots, single and double, and I feel that it is generous of the swami to give me this *nihil obstat*. The experience I describe is that of Raja Yoga, the purely intellectual approach to the discovery of the true self, and I describe the path as long and hard. For me, it was. Rajneesh's own thinking is firmly based on the austere principles of the original sages, as my own is. But he has invented a simpler way of at least getting a glimpse of what the original sages were talking about. I think it interesting, practical, and spectacular.

In my book*, I describe how, during my experiment, I was quite alone. This is perhaps not so trying for a writer as it would be for others: he spends most of his day alone. But Rajneesh saw that it was fear of loneliness that made people seek him out, as thousands do. He therefore invented 'mass meditation'. I have attended one of these sessions, not to meditate, but to observe.

It took place at 9 a.m. under the dazzling, but still tolerable, morning sun of India. The site was a large open space, the garden of some institution unconnected with Rajneesh. There was nothing very private about the garden: a wall bounded one side of it on which were perched urchins and fisherboys ready to watch the

The Space Within the Heart.

201

< The swami Bhagwan Shree Rajneesh
beginning a session of mass meditation.

Bhagwan Shree Rajneesh.

fun. When I arrived, on time, it already held some two thousand people. The entrance fee was nominal – 12 cents – which was not always collected.

On a platform at one end was a revolving chair, covered in fawn leather. It was a luxurious affair, of the sort that one would expect to find behind the huge desk of some top American executive. On this chair sat the swami, relaxed as no top executive ever is. He gazed at the audience as though there was nobody at all. It was composed mostly of Indians – clerks on their way to the office, housewives on their way to the shops, some neatly suited businessmen, university students, and a few old men in retirement. There were some foreigners, Americans and Swedes in the main, and a scattering of those young people in scanty Indian dress who come from abroad, seeking wisdom. I saw no Dharma-bums or their successors. All sat on the ground, with a fringe of standing people who, like me, were interested spectators.

A little group of women carried a parcel to the dais, unwrapped it, and showed it briefly to the swami. It was a plaster model of his feet, gilded, and intended, I was told, for some South American ashram. Then the mass meditation began.

Speaking first in Hindi and then in excellent English, the swami told us with the utmost brevity what was going to happen. For the first twenty minutes the audience was to let itself go. 'Do exactly what you like: shout, dance, sing: just as you please. For the next twenty minutes meditate in absolute silence: meditate on whatever you choose. I shall be here to help you. For the last twenty minutes be happy: let me dance in your hearts.'

I noted particularly that in his whole brief address – he made no other – only this last sentence had any touch of rhetoric. This was a rare thing in India, where to speak in public without lengthy preambles, turgid prose and portentous but empty similes is considered almost an insult to the public.

A brisk rhythm from an expert drummer (on tape, the machine being clearly visible together with a worried recording engineer) roared from powerful loud speakers. For a few moments nobody moved. Then the swami swivelled his chair round to the left. He held out his hands, palm upwards, fingers wide apart. His head leaned gently to one side, in a gesture of gentle, almost feminine, invitation. Slowly he swivelled round a full half-circle. As he moved, pandemonium broke out under his abstracted gaze.

I have seen hysteria in crowds. I have followed the fortunes of an Italian boxer in Rome from his beginnings to the time when he became world champion and the Romans made so much noise they would have terrified lions in the Colosseum: I have attended Nazi rallies: but I have never seen anything like this. People were shouting, singing, and performing the most extraordinary actions all over the

Rajneesh invites his audience to do whatever they please as the first stage of mass meditation.

place, but there was absolutely no sense of a crowd. Each person acted completely on his own, glancing neither right nor left. Some followed with their eyes the man with upraised hands who was slowly, very slowly, turning on his chair: many did not. His tranquil expression, the controlled beauty of his gesture, was a pleasure to watch, but there was no magnetism about it. As for me, I thought of a play by Sophocles performed in classic style, where the actors spoke lines filled with passion from behind immobile masks. The contrast between the swami and his audience had something of the same effect.

One man flung his arms repeatedly in the air, singing tunelessly. Another danced round and round, a beatific expression on his face, not with the hop, skip and a jump of the Hare Krishna-ites, but with graceful, ballroom steps. He was dancing, I thought, with the girl of his dreams. Another young man took off his jacket, and with jabs of his right and left fists fought an invisible antagonist with all the joy of a boxer punching his way to victory. An American woman, grey-haired, squatted on the ground with her eyes closed, clapping her hands with voluptuous movements. A man who was obviously an office clerk, stripped

The second stage: meditation in absolute silence.

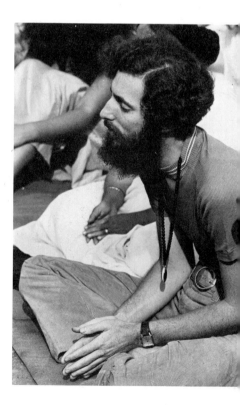

his coat, shirt and vest, and stood, immobile, clad only in his flimsy dhoti. At his feet a man flung himself on the ground and rolled about there, like a child on a soft carpet. A pretty girl gyrated slowly, her hands in a seductive gesture, as though she were a fashion-model. One old woman turned her face to the sky, weeping profusely and laughing at the same time. From all over, as the drum pulsed without stop, came a confused sound of voices as people shouted meaning-less syllables. Nobody, as far as I could hear, was chanting a mantra. To the rhythm of the drum one man gave violent jerks of his head, left, right, left, right, till I thought he would break his neck.

The drum stopped. Everybody stood or sat still. 'Now,' said the swami, 'twenty minutes of meditation. Be still, be silent, close your eyes.' A hush spread across the assembly, which deepened into complete silence. The noises of the city crept back into my consciousness. Some people closed their eyes, others just stared into vacancy. The boxer relaxed his muscles visibly, the frantic dancers sat in utter stillness. There were no whispered prayers, no yoga postures, no mystic gestures of finger and thumb. Only stillness and a great quiet.

Rajneesh: 'Twenty minutes of meditation. Be still, be silent, close your eyes.'

The third stage: a renewal of movement, followed by exhaustion.

The drum started again, a softer, tripping rhythm this time. 'Now,' said the swami, 'joy. Let us be happy.' The dancers got to their feet and danced but without frenzy. The boxer stood up, spread his arms, and smiled. The man who had rolled on the ground, stretched himself, still lying horizontal, and laughed. The pretty girl composed her face into an infant's smile. The man who had stripped half-naked rubbed his torso admiringly.

The drum stopped for the last time. The swami left his chair and moved to his car, people crowding round him to touch his hands or feet. Assistants moved his chair and put it on the top of a taxi. The swami drove away. An American girl burst into violent sobbing, while her companions watched her with amused smiles. The place of assembly was dotted with prone men and women, exhausted by their experience.

One of the most notable things at the meeting was the respectability of the response to the invitation, 'Do what you like.' Carnival-time in a Catholic country invariably sees some sights that cause raised eyebrows in even the broad-minded: so much so that Carnival is forbidden in Rome because it might shock the pilgrims. But this criticism is not quite fair to Swami Rajneesh. The mass-meditation I saw was in a big city. Nudity (for instance) is forbidden within city precincts, even to fakirs. When Rajneesh holds his meetings in more secluded places such as the holy hill called Mount Abu, some of his followers strip naked with all the nonchalance of Western actors and actresses.

His invitation to freedom should not be taken with undue gravity. It is more like packing the kids off to the swimming hole for the summer afternoon. What is remarkable and new is the second twenty minutes. Whether the audience really meditates or not I cannot say. I can confirm that after the drumming and the frenzy there is that sort of silence which only a great solo musician can command. Even he could not produce that utter stillness: no coughing, no fidgeting. Like the soloist, Rajneesh is there on the platform, gyrating in his chair. But a large number of those in an enviable state of calm relaxation were not even looking at

An old woman experiences ecstasy in the second stage of Rajneesh's meeting.

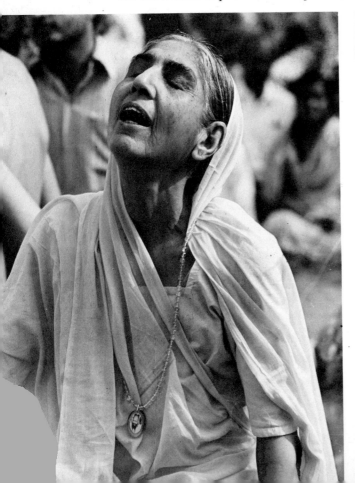

him. I have heard John Kennedy address a joint session of Congress, my seat being to his right behind him, so that I could observe the audience. He did not produce the stillness of Rajneesh, except from the Justices of the Supreme Court. But they were sitting in the front row, right underneath him and they had longer experience in suppressing yawns and the furtive scratch.

Nevertheless, Rajneesh's meeting was a public show, as much as those of Billy Graham, though mercifully less verbose. In private, he is close to the true teachings of the Upanishads. He is at pains to point out that to gain the knowledge of the real self, one must be alone. Like the sages, he attacks society in words that are a good deal sharper than those of Marcuse:

'Every type of social institution is a means to kill the individual and convert him into a machine. All our universities are factories to kill the spontaneous – to kill the spark, to kill the spirit and change man into a machine. Then society feels at ease with him. He can be relied upon. He can be predicted. Man becomes predictable as soon as he becomes a machine. We can predict a husband, a wife, a lawyer, a scientist. We know who they are and how they will react. We can be at ease with them.'

He argues that we are all too rational, a philosophical word which is a little too worn to have much meaning. He has improved upon it. He says we *over-do*. 'In the world in which you are proficient', he says, 'you tend to over-do. This over-doing is the problem. One must not be an expert all the twenty-four hours. One must also do something in which one is no-one. One must also do something about which one knows nothing. One must be a child, playing sometimes, immature, unknowing, ignorant.'

It recalls Ramakrishna asking Vivekananda to explain 'logic' and then not waiting for an answer.

At the end of the mass meditation, Rajneesh leaves, guarded by a policeman from the throng. He blesses a handkerchief.

Chinmayananda

We are near the end of our journey, and the end can be only one thing: to find a man who honestly echoes the words of the sages of the Upanishads with which we began. There are very few of them. I select Swami Chinmayananda, without prejudice to the rest of the few.

He is a tall man, middle-aged but full of vigour. He has fine Southern Indian features partly concealed by a beard such as you find on antique Greek busts. He has a rich voice and a keen mind. His real name – as he reminded me within seconds of our meeting – is Nair, meaning that he belongs to the same caste-division as my father.

He is described by his rivals as 'the intellectual's swami', and that does very well for me. I do not deny that we should all be, sometimes, as little children. I even practise it. Here on my desk I have a box of children's building bricks. When the swamis get unbearably prolix in their writings I put them aside and build castles, and I consign the prolix swamis to the lowest dungeon. But the Upanishads can be described as an intellectual exercise to end all intellectual exercises, in the literal meaning of those words. Therefore Chinmayananda suits me.

In our journey along the path, I am sure that the reader must have felt that we have looked down many strange byways, especially where the worship of the gods came in, or, as it is called, Bhakti.

Here is Chinmayananda on the subject. He is explaining a sentence of Sankara in which there is some measured criticism of it.

Sankara cannot be criticised, at least not by those who understand what he says. Bhakti, as it has come down to us to-day, represents almost a superstitious conception, stinking in its decadence, a moral dread, a disgusting intellectual slavery, a crawling mental attitude, a blind dependence on a supreme God, to take us away from all our self-created mischiefs. So we find a self-ruined society being courted by a profit-seeking priest-class, functioning generally from spiritually-polluted centres which have come to be called 'temples'. Those who visit these polluted centres are found to be a set of helpless personalities with neither the courage to face life nor the conviction to renounce, neither the mental stamina to live, nor the intellectual vigour to enquire, neither the imagination to believe nor the daring to disbelieve – they are mainly a crowd of people flocking towards the sanctum – half in fear and half in deluded hopes.

I do not think that Chinmayananda is directly attacking the Hare Krishna movement, which is just as well, because their ashram lies only a mile or two down the road from his, and both have some sturdy young students. But he *is* attacking the excesses of facile emotion which some aspects of Hinduism have shown and from which the mystics are not altogether free. His criticism of some schools of Yoga is more direct.

'Yoga is nowadays greatly misunderstood by Eastern and Western book readers. They think that Yoga means some occult powers and superhuman strength of the bodies and senses. They never practise Yoga for the realisation of the Self.'

Swami Chinmayananda in repose and talking to disciples.

For Chinmayananda the study of the Upanishads and the Gita is enough. He says, like the original sages, 'Sit down beside me.' Every summer, ten thousand people do so, day after day. There are no thrones, no drums, and above all, no hair-splitting. When he comes to a passage which has an awkward message he does not dodge it: he stresses it. He is a Sanskrit scholar, but (and this is rare in that company) he is a completely honest one. He has published translations and comments on eleven Upanishads: they do not make much pretension to literary grace, but reading them you can be sure that you are hearing what the sages said.

There is a book* by Sankara which for centuries has been considered the best summing-up of what the Upanishads are about. Here is Chinmayananda translating and explaining its crucial passages. In one of them a pupil is being advised by a sage that if he wishes to discover his real self he must (as we have seen) free himself from all attachment.

'Conquer this great infatuation for your body, wife, children and so forth,' says the text. And Chinmayananda hammers its point home: he explains the text word for word:

'Wife (dara) is to be understood as not only the wedded partner in life. In [Hindu] philosophy, the word often indicates all those on whom you depend for your happiness. Sons (Suta) stand for all those who depend on you. As an individual I exist in society looking up to people who make me happy, looking after those who turn to me for their comforts. In the language of the spiritual Masters, "wife, children" is an idiom that includes all those relationships.'

This is quite true. But Chinmayananda need not have said it. Many swamis would drop the whole passage: 'Selections from . . .' is a very convenient title. Others would have wrapped it up in rhetoric, especially when talking to wives. Chinmayananda goes on with his commentary:

'In the midst of all these webs of relationships an individual exists, maintaining different types of intimate attachments which have a knack of expanding their thraldom. Suffocated by these, he gets exhausted. This is the death of all spiritual aspirations of the seeker.'

I know of no clearer explanation of why the sages of the Upanishads appeal, more and more, to the modern world.

Chinmayananda is not himself a cold man: on the contrary, his personality is warm and cheerful. He likes a joke and makes many of his own. His ashram is a pretty place with pink buildings set among flowering trees. It is not a place for people to strip off their clothing and dance away their repressions. It is a place for

*The *Vivekachoodamani*; See short bibliography at the end of this book.

Chinmayananda explains the Gita to an open-air meeting.

quiet study. His disciples sign on for a course which lasts five years in which they will analyse the Upanishads, the Gita and Sankara, line by line, under Chinmayananda's guidance. There is a temple for those who do not wish to tear themselves away too quickly from the faith of their fathers, but in it there are no hysterical scenes of religious devotion. There are no miraculous cures either: going up steps, Chinmayananda will pause and tell the visitor that he has had a heart-attack and must suffer it, just like you and me.

He claims no rare powers, but he has got one – sanity. That, when all is said and done, is what the sages were looking for in a world which, like ours, was fast becoming preposterous.

Chinmayananda's ashram in Bombay: (left above) the dome of the modern temple is in the shape of a lingam; (left) the bull Nandi looks into the temple; (above) a disciple rings the temple bell at sunset.

The modern statue of Shiva in Chinmayananda's ashram is an aid to meditation for orthodox Hindus, but does not form a part of the mystic instruction.

The swami talks happily to a disciple.

A concluding example

I began this enquiry with a fictitious housewife. I shall end with a real one. The first found no solution to her problem, only the Snake on a Caribbean island. The second has succeeded. She is a very happy woman, in spite of the fact that her husband has divorced her.

She is Dutch. She has the broad features of that race, and the subdued manner. She was born and bred in Holland and, till the revolution in her life, had never been outside its borders, nor had she any wish to go. She married a Colonial, and it was a mild union, in the Dutch manner. He had no interests outside his profession, which was that of a chemical engineer, while she had no interests outside her house and family. She was not religious, she did not read books, she had no hobbies or cultural interests. She had a kind heart, and broad shoulders for the children to cry on. They had three, all girls. It would have needed the brush of Vermeer to find anything romantic in her.

She had two sisters, who turned to her in their troubles, and they both had plenty. One had made a marriage which ended unhappily. The other was widowed and left with no money. Both came to live with her, with their respective offspring. Her father-in-law had a cancerous condition, and he came to live with her, too. In all there were, at one time, eleven people living under her roof. She did not resent this, but plainly she had no time which she could call her own. If at times she felt a weariness of her fate, she put that down to a chronic anaemia from which she suffered.

When she was in her forties, one of her relatives brought an Indian swami to the house. He liked the place and added himself to the family. Lily (for that was her name) cooked for him along with the others but without the same easy affection. He was, in the first place, fussy about his food: she had to clear up after the audiences he gave to the curious, and in the third place, he had the brazenness to ask her if she could type. She said she could, so, with his blessings, he gave her a pile of secretarial work. With all this, it is not surprising that she took a poor view of Indian mysticism.

But she thought about it. The swami's discourses were above her head, and he knew it. He made no attempt to draw her into his following, except as an unpaid cook-housekeeper-typist. Yet something of that wind of freedom that is found in the Upanishads became to play upon her mind. She meditated.

Then one day she announced to an astounded household that she had decided what she was going to do. She was going to become a sannyasi, one, that is, who renounces the usual things of the world and goes out in search of the truth. Vivekandanda was a sannyasi when he went on his first tour of India.

If the swami-in-residence thought that he had made a useful disciple, he was soon disillusioned. Lily said she had no intention of staying in the house. She was going to India.

It would be fine and dramatic if I could say that she forthwith donned the saffron robe and walked out of the house. But Mrs Lily Eversdijk-Smulders was a real woman. She faced a storming family row. She was told she musn't do it, she couldn't do it, and what would they do without her? She meditated anew and came up smilingly with an answer. They must do the best they could. Father-in-law was now dragged into the fray. He was a very sick man. She had nursed him for a long time. How could she leave him in his extremity? This gave her pause. Her practical chemical engineering husband came in with a clincher. To go to India she would need at least a thousand dollars. Where was the money coming from?

She stayed. She did her duty as a wife, mother, sister, and daughter-in-law, and typist. She had always done it. But now (she admits) she did it with a neutral detachment. She was, in a word, following the advice of the sages of the Upanishads and the Gita, though she knew little about the texts of either. Meditation – amateur meditation, if you will – had led her to this point.

The father-in-law duly died of his cancer. Lily had obeyed what is perhaps the supreme, the ineluctable imperative – to comfort the dying. Freed from this bond, she felt freed from all the lesser ones. She repeated her decision to go, and friends, awed by her constancy, raised the money in dribs and drabs.

The swami-in-residence, stoically facing the loss of a cook-secretary, bestirred himself. Lily did not know India: the swami did. He was certain that Lily would not be able to look after herself there. He advised her to take her teen-aged daughter with her as a companion. She agreed. She bought the air-tickets. She went to the airport. The whole household was there to see her off. What happened there must be described in her own words.

'They were weeping. I felt sad that they were weeping, but I did not weep myself. I only knew I was *going*. I did not know what I was going to, but it did not matter. I loved them all as much as I had ever done, but that did not matter either. I really knew nothing about the world outside Holland and my home, so I was not afraid of anything. It was all just a bit comic. I was so ignorant that I thought that the air-conditioning in the plane was just ordinary air. When I stepped out of the cabin into the heat of Delhi airport, I was shocked. I thought I was walking into an oven. No. I didn't think, "This is India, at last!" I had no emotions about India at all. The swami had written to some people to meet me. There they were, and very soon I knew they thought the way I did, though nobody said anything very much. So I stayed in India. That was six years ago, and here I still am.'

The husband who had been thus so strangely deserted, behaved in the pragmatical manner to be expected of a chemical engineer. He did not reprove her or ask her to come back. After a due interval he sent her papers for divorce, which she duly signed. They were divorced. He married again.

One speculates on that second marriage. The husband had lost not only a wife but also a daughter. The girl, like her mother, went her own way and became a sannyasi. The second wife must have been sympathetic to her husband's unusual troubles: second wives always are. But what did she think when her husband, after a while, began to study Yoga?

Lily learned Sanskrit, or as much of it as a middle-aged Dutch housewife could. She changed her name to that of the swami Yogeshwarananda. She teaches a very mild form of Yoga, more because her pupils want something to *do*, rather than just *think*. But the nub of her teaching is meditation, since meditation, untrained and undisciplined, was the beginning of her new life. Just as she made no fuss about a household of eleven people, her view of meditation is undramatic.

'You can meditate anytime, anywhere,' she tells her pupils, as do all the genuine teachers of the Upanishads. But she adds something peculiarly her own. 'And when you do,' she says, 'Home is just where you are.'

Religion still dominates the daily round in India. Vedanta has had a deep effect;
here a girl washes her feet before private worship.

Appendix: Zen

In recent years there has been, in America, a rapid growth of interest in Zen. The reason is plain. In those same recent years Americans, on a world scale, have again and again plunged into action without thought of the consequences; sometimes, in truth, without any thought at all.

That is the essence and nub of the teachings of Zen – action without using the rational faculties, which the believer destroys in himself by submitting to a series of mental disciplines which often run to the bizarre.

Zen is a sect of Buddhism, and at this point it is convenient to point out that Buddhism, in India, has virtually ceased to exist. There are a few scattered monasteries, largely frequented by foreigners or visiting Buddhists from abroad. The three million Buddhists who show in the census figures form only 0.74 per cent of India's huge population. Of these, the majority are not really believers. They are Untouchables who have chosen 'conversion' to show their anger with orthodox Hindus, who, in spite of the law, still persecute them in the remoter parts of the countryside.

Tradition has it that Zen was brought to China by an Indian Buddhist monk called Bodhidharma. He is portrayed as a fierce-eyed, shouting bully, a curious character for a Buddhist. There is considerable doubt as to whether he ever existed, for there are no records of him in Indian Buddhist writings. He is said to have arrived in Canton in AD 480 at the invitation of the Emperor of China, a devout Buddhist. The Emperor showed the monk the temples, monasteries and so forth that he had built and humbly asked him what merit he had attained. 'None!' Bodhidharma roared at him. Retiring from the court, Bodhidharma spent many years in a monastery, gazing at a blank wall.

Zen masters (as adepts are called) insist that Zen cannot be described in words, for which they have great contempt. Slaps and blows with a stick are preferred methods of instructing pupils, or sending them on pointless errands. The substance of their teachings is, however, not at all mysterious, and can be described in modern medical terms.

The human brain has two parts – the top lobes which is called the cortex, and a bottom portion, just behind the top of the neck, which is the cerebellum. Thinking is done by the cortex: our instinctive actions have their source in the cerebellum. The teachers of Zen condemn the cortex and highly value the cerebellum, in which resides, they say, a man's true self. A student once approached a famous Zen master and asked him to tell him what Zen was. The master refused, and sent the student away. As the young man was going through the door, the master called out his name. The student stopped, turned and said, 'Yes?' '*There* it is,' said the master.

Medically speaking, both parts of the brain had played a part in that action, but as the master did not know of the existence of either, it does not matter: the story admirably illustrates the Zen desire for spontaneous action. When the action of the cortex is repressed as far as possible, the Zen adept arrives at a state called *satori*. It has been compared by one master to a feeling of walking on air. The sensation is usually described as being one full of 'bliss', and it may be more closely defined as a state of liberation.

It should be noted that this state has nothing to do with the self-examination and final tranquillity of the Upanishads. Zen does not permit the long, rational study of the self, the peeling of the onion. Nor is the end result tranquil. The Zen master laughs, shouts, has fits of irrational anger and generally behaves (as they say) like a happy madman. At only one point does Zen touch the Upanishads: in both doctrines you attain a state of pure awareness of things, without judging them.

Since Zen cannot be learned from books, it is necessary to acquire it from a master. Since he can use words only sparingly, these being too cortical, other methods have to be used. One of these, since it has no parallel elsewhere, must be called by its technical name, the *Koan*. It is a sort of game in which the pupil is tempted to use his brains, and then made a fool of for doing so. With all respect to the Zen masters, I think one of the best *Koans* is a party game I played – or had played on me – as a child. A row of bottles is placed on the floor: the child is blindfolded and invited to step carefully over each successive bottle without knocking them over. Loud shouts of approval accompany him as he, apparently, succeeds. The child, proud of his skill, takes off the blindfold. He then sees that the bottles have all been removed before he started.

As will be seen from that example, *Koans* must be kept secret. But some have become famous. Of these, the following are typical. The master says to the pupil: 'A girl is walking down the road. Is she the older or the younger sister?' The pupil struggles to answer the question (an experiment on your friends will show that they always do). He gives up. The master then rises and walks across the room with a swaying gait like the girl. The object of this lesson is to teach the pupil not to bother his head with questions about the girl's relations, but to see her as just plain *girl*, with all her girlishness.

In another *Koan*, the master asks the pupil: 'When the bath water goes down the plug hole, does it go in a clockwise or anti-clockwise direction?' The correct answer is to say nothing at all, but to raise a finger in the air and waggle it round and round in either direction indifferently.

The instruction takes place in monasteries, presided over by a master, who, on occasion, puts on ceremonial robes. At all times, he holds himself aloof from the pupil, endeavouring to strike him with awe. The student also risks being struck with something more material: during meditation periods, attendants circulate with rods which they lay across the shoulders of pupils who are sleeping or slouching. Hard work in running and cleaning the monasteries is part of the discipline, which also includes worship of the Buddha in rituals conducted with great pomp and magnificence. Zen masters insist that Zen is a strictly non-religious belief: how this can be reconciled with religious ceremonies is a moot question, so unanswerable that it is almost a *Koan*. Initiates reply that the show is well worth watching.

Zen originated in China, but when the Japanese began importing Chinese culture in the early Middle Ages, Zen took root in Japan and flourished. Its cult of spontaneous action greatly appealed to the aggressive knightly order known as the Samurai, while, on a less bloodthirsty plane, its advocacy of simple aware-ness influenced Japanese painting and poetry.

But many followers of Zen deplore this later elaboration. In its origin, Zen was simplistic, no belief more so. In the words of Lin-chi (died 867): 'There is no place in Buddhism for using effort. Just be ordinary and nothing special. Relieve your bowels, pass water, put on your clothes and eat your food. When you're tired, go and lie down. Ignorant people may laugh at me, but the wise will understand.'

Books for further reading

Index

Books for further reading

BHAKTIVEDANTA, A. C., *Krishna Consciousness*.

BRIGGS, G. W., *Goraknath and the Kanphata Yogis*, London, 1938.

CHINMAYANANDA, SWAMI, *Talks on Sankara's Vivekachoodamani*.

CHINMAYANANDA, SWAMI, *Kathopanishad*.

HIRIYANNA, M., *The Essentials of Indian Philosophy*, London, 1932.

HUME, R. E., *The Thirteen Principal Upanishads,* Oxford, 1921.

ISHERWOOD, CHRISTOPHER, *Ramakrishna and his Disciples*, London, 1965.

IYENGAR, B. K. S., *Light on Yoga: Yoga Dipika*, London, 1968.

KRISHNAMURTI, JIDDU, *Commentaries on Living*, London, 1956.

KRISHNAMURTI, JIDDU, *Freedom from the Known*, London, 1969.

MAJUMDAR, RAMESA-CHANDRA and others, *An Advanced History of India*, London, 1950.

MAJUMDAR, RAMESA-CHANDRA, *The Vedic Age*.

MURPHET, HOWARD, *Sai Baba*, London, 1971.

NEHRU, JAWAHARLAL, *An Autobiography*, London, 1936; new edition 1942.

NEVIDITA, SISTER and numerous others, *Reminiscences of Swami Vivekananda*.

PRABHAVANDANDA, SWAMI, *Vedic Religion and Philosophy*, Mylapore, 1937.

RADHAKRISHNAN, SARVEPALLI, *The Principal Upanishads*, London, 1953.

RADHAKRISHNAN, SARVEPALLI, *The Bhagavad Gita*, London, 1948.

RAJNEESH, ACHARYA, *Mysteries of Life and Death*.

ROLLAND, ROMAIN, *The Life of Vivekananda*, London, 1930.

SARKAR, JADUNATH, *Chaitanya and his Age*.

SMITH, VINCENT, *The Oxford History of India*, Oxford, 1919; revised 1923.

SUZUKI, D. T., *Essays on Zen Buddhism*, London, 1970.

SUZUKI, D. T., *An introduction to Zen Buddhism*, London, 1969.

WALKER, BENJAMIN, *Hindu World, An Encyclopedic Survey of Hinduism*, London, 1968.

WOODROFFE, JOHN, *Principles of Tantra*.

YOGENDRA, SHRI, *Yoga Essays*.

Index